FROM THE SHADOWS

Being Alone is the Hardest Part of Loss

George Samerjan

DEDICATION

For my grandson, Tucker Simmons, who inspired the story from our many trips into the Adirondacks.
George Samerjan

CONTENTS

ACKNOWLEDGMENTS

The author gratefully thanks the following for their help, support, and encouragement.

John Silbersack - agent and reviewer who provided invaluable counsel before and during the writing of this novel

And Happy - who patiently abided during writing days

CHAPTER 1

ASSAULT

Jim looked up from his monotonous task of weighing and bundling marijuana into cellophane bags at the rough hewn table in the ramshackle cabin. He stared through the filthy plastic sheet window of the cabin at the yellow, flickering light of a campfire across the river appearing in contrast to nightfall.

"Snuff the lights, we got company, boys. Let's check it out."

Jim tossed on a dirty jacket, and looked at Dan and Mike.

"Can't be the law. Law isn't stupid enough to get this close and light a fire. Campers don't come in this far unless they're real lost. We never had anybody this lost before. Let's go."

Jim shook his head.

"I thought the stories were enough to keep most people out."

The three men picked up AK47's, checked magazines to insure they contained rounds, inserted them into the automatic rifles, and pulled the charging levers back. They let the bolts slam forward to chamber a round, and then exited the cabin. Jim led the other two quietly through a field thick with tall marijuana plants festooned with carefully placed booby traps.

Pale olive camouflage nets were strung between the trees. The nets blocked out a view down from directly above, but allowed sunlight to come in at an angle and reach the plants.

Silently the three men slowly approached the fast moving bank of the Gunpowder River. Jim motioned to the others to move downstream out of sight of whoever was at the fire. Their passage muffled by the water, three, dark shapes bent low to the rushing white water made the crossing and reached the other bank. They pulled themselves up the bank with one hand while carrying their rifles in the other hand. They paused for a moment to catch their breaths.

"Take her slow boys. First we want to see what we got here."

They made their way to the camp without making a sound and crouched behind a massive fallen log. Only their hair matted with sweat and river water, foreheads, and eyes rose above the rotting bark of the log.

Jim smiled menacingly.

"Well, if it ain't our old friend, John Pierce," he whispered grinning.

"His wife, and that kid they been raising."

"That kid is the one who…" Mike said.

"But we…" Dan added.

"I told you two to never to talk about that," Jim snapped.

He shook his head. "Even out here, among us. Never. They're a long way from anywhere. Pinched me once for taking a deer out of season."

"Think they saw the fields?" Mike asked.

"We can't take that chance," Jim replied. "I got two strikes, and I ain't spending the rest of my life behind bars because of him. He's a real straight shooter. He sees the fields in the morning he'll go back and report it. A ton of law will show up here. The three of us will be making little rocks out of big rocks for the rest of our lives."

He paused for effect.

"Or, they'll roll up our sleeves and shoot us full of some lethal cocktail."

Mike and Dan looked down at the ground, to each other, and then back to Jim. They were more afraid of Jim than they were of the consequences of their actions.

Jim pointed to Mike and then to Amanda. Her back was to them as she slept in her sleeping bag. Her long, blonde hair shone in the firelight. Jim pointed to Dan, and then to the shape in the smaller sleeping bag.

"That's the boy, Dan. You boys get the woman and the boy. I'll take care of Pierce."

"We got to kill the woman and kid, too?" Dan asked.

Jim slid back down the log, and pulled his two men alongside him.

"Do the math," he said grasping their shirts. "We leave them alive we got witnesses to a murder. We don't kill them and they report the field, we're going away for a long, long time. Think about it."

He paused.

"You want to die in prison?"

"I ain't killed no one before," Dan said. "That ain't my line. Drugs, stealin', not killin'."

"Mike killed that dealer with that gun you bought. You're in just as deep as he is. You will be in this, even if you don't do nothin', and you will do somethin'. You don't have a choice."

Jim's eyes glared ferociously at Dan with a clear message.

"It's them or it's me and you."

Jim raised the barrel of his AK47.

"Right here, right now. What is it?"

Dan nodded.

"All right, let's do it."

Jim, Mike, and Dan separated and crawled through the woods toward the still glowing fire. Each man had a long bladed hunting knife in his hand.

Tucker was fifteen years old. He had sandy blonde hair in a usually unkempt state, and blue eyes. He was nearly six feet tall, and was athletic. His eyes heavy with sleep, he rose from the sleeping bag with a flashlight and headed into the nearby woods to urinate. The light of the flashlight bounced up and down in rhythm to the swing of his hand and the trod of his feet. He went back down the trail several yards before stepping into the knee high brush. The wind in the trees made a rustling sound like waves lapping against a shore. Once he was done he retraced his steps back toward the campsite. His head was down watching the trail in the yellow light of the flashlight. He was barely awake.

Jim paused deep in shadow inches away from John and nodded to Mike who was perched over Amanda as if he were a bird of prey. As one, Jim and Mike locked John and Amanda's heads in a headlock with their left arms jolting their victims from sleep to alertness. In a stunned instant, their victims' eyes upon them and before either John or Amanda could resist, Jim and Dan brought the razor sharp blades down hard, slashing their victim's throats nearly to the spine. Released by the killers, blood and white foam streaming from their slit throats, John and Amanda collapsed in convulsions, and then went still.

Nearby, Dan held up Tucker's empty sleeping bag. The three men looked up at the sight of a flashlight beam coming toward them, and saw Tucker emerge from the shadows of the trail into the firelight. Tucker raised his flashlight casting a bright white spotlight on the bodies of his grandparents. Tucker's hand shook causing the oval beam to dance across the bodies.

Tucker saw strangers kneeling over John and Amanda's blood soaked, lifeless bodies. The men crouched with knives in their hands. Blood dripped from the tips of the blades like drops from the teeth of a carnivore.

Tucker suddenly realized that he was standing frozen out of disbelief and fear, and the killers were looking at him.

Run! Run somewhere fast and get away from these men! Hide!

Tucker turned, threw the flashlight away, and ran headlong into the woods. Part of him knew how dangerous it was to run through unknown woods at night without any knowledge of what lay before him, but another part of him urged him to run as fast as he could away from these men. Grandpa John had taught him not to panic in the woods, but Tucker knew he had to get away from these men before he could think of anything else.

Tucker ran frantically through the woods, limbs slapping his face and brush clutching at his arms and legs. Confusion and fear overwhelmed him. He felt as if he had to tell his legs to keep running. Behind him he heard the sounds of large men tramping through the brush. The sound gave him strength to run even harder. Around him, three oval patterns of light darted through the night across the black woods seeking him.

Stay out of the lights.

He heard them smashing through the brush behind him. Something unseen by Tucker took form beneath the thick foliage. It caused a furrow in its wake.

Tucker scrambled up the hillside. His fingers dug into the damp earth. Fighting with all his strength, he clawed his way against the thick brush, and the damp cold earth. There were bloody scratches on his face and tears in his clothing. He didn't know where he was going. They had never been in this far before and they'd never been off this trail. Tucker's arms and legs began to cramp. He felt a jagged pain in his right side. His throat was parched and his lungs were hot with pain. Still, Tucker kept moving further into the woods away from the trail.

Dan stopped fifty yards away from the trail at the base of the ridge panting for breath. He angled his flashlight at the path of broken brush leading into the woods. Jim and Mike surveyed the thick woods around them as they cast the beams of their flashlights across the forest. Jim stared up the slope while Dan and Mike watched and waited.

"Kid is fast."

Jim tried to catch his breath.

"What'll we do?" asked Dan, "What'll we do?"

"Just wait a goddamn minute!" shouted Jim. "I've got to think."

The woods on both sides of the track left by Tucker were almost impenetrable. Jim paced back and forth for a moment. Jim's flashlight beam stayed directed on the trail.

A howl, like that of a wolf, but somehow different, came from the darkness. Jim, Mike, and Dan stepped closer together, back to back, knives thrust out before them. They searched the darkness with their flashlights. Their minds conjured up unwelcome images of what creature howled before them. Nearby branches rustled sharply, and then stopped. Yards away, branches rustled again. A second howl came, louder now. A third howl came from behind them. Then, a pair of brilliant red eyes glowed in the darkness on the ridge before them on the path leading to Tucker.

"I don't know what the hell this is. We're getting the hell out of here," announced Jim. "That's what we're doing."

"What about the boy?" said Dan, "He seen everything."

"We aren't going to find him at night. He can't get far tonight, and I ain't dealin' with whatever the hell that is. Not at night. We'll come back in the morning when we can track him."

Jim glanced up at the ridge, and then took a deep breath.

"All right, you two, let's get rid of those bodies. Saw some bear tracks on the other side of the stream. Look recent. Let the bears take care of the mess, and whatever else will scavenge. A few weeks from now there won't be a trace."

Dan and Mike started back down the trail. Jim watched them leave, and then looked one more time up the hill. The spine chilling howl came again. It seemed to be not far off. A set of red eyes on the ridge above looked down upon Jim. For an instant he stared at the penetrating red eyes, and then he turned and quickly caught up to the others.

He collected all of the camping gear stuffing it into two sleeping bags. He lugged the gear behind him down the trail. Reaching the riverbank he dropped the two bags, and then went back to the murder site. He stripped a branch with leaves from a tree, and then backed down the trail to the riverbank erasing his tracks as he went.

Dan and Mike lifted the bodies of John and Amanda, carried them across the stream to where they'd seen the bear tracks, dumped them on the ground, and then headed back to their shack.

Pausing on the far bank Jim looked back to where he would start the hunt for the boy in the morning.

CHAPTER 2

ALONE

Tucker ran headlong through the pitch-black woods. Terror fueled his flailing passage through the brush and branches. Branches slapped at his face and arms. Sweat caused the scratches on his face and arms to burn.

It seemed to Tucker that the forest was scheming with the murderers to slow his escape. Tucker didn't know if the killers were still chasing him or not, but he decided to run until he couldn't run any longer. He couldn't hear them anymore, but that didn't mean that they weren't sneaking up on him.

Tucker paused for a moment, reached out, and clung to a narrow tree trunk with his right hand.

What if they split up? What if one of them is moving around me?

Fear put a cold, hard rock in Tucker's stomach. He couldn't see. The killers could be within reach and he wouldn't know it until it was too late. Then, he thought of the John and Amanda. Tucker shivered. He almost cried out at the pain in his left thigh. Like an invisible fist, the cramp took the muscle in his thigh and twisted it into a knot the size of a lemon. Tucker reached down with his right hand and pulled and pressed at the spasm. Leaning against the tree he angled his toe and stretched his leg.

His cotton polo shirt and blue jeans were soaked with sweat. His sock clad feet were wet and caked with mud. His hair was matted with sweat. He had bloody scratches on his forearms and hands.

He continued kneading the cramp until it was gone. He thought he should have gone back for his sneakers, but then he thought how stupid that was. They would have gotten him. Then, he thought how stupid it was to be thinking those things at all. He couldn't see. He had to think. He had to think before he did something stupid and got hurt. If he got hurt they would be on him. He had to get through this night, get some distance from the killers, and find his way out. Then, he could get the police and bring them back in here. But, first, he had to survive. He had to keep going.

Tucker listened as hard as he could over the sound of his breathing and the pounding of his heart in his ears. He did not hear anything moving behind him. Perhaps they'd given up for now.

Tucker sensed that he had reached the crest of a ridge. He couldn't see it, but he felt the transition from the ridge to flat ground. The forest canopy prevented the starlight from reaching down to the forest floor.

He slowed his pace. He would be more cautious now if they weren't close behind him. He took a deep breath, and then as he stepped forward his feet suddenly no longer touched the ground. Flailing out with his hands and feet he felt nothing but air, and knew he was falling. He feared whatever waited in the darkness for him, and then it all went black as his body struck stone.

An unseen shape with a pair of red eyes hovered at the edge of the precipice looking down on Tucker in the bottom of the ravine, circled, and then nestled in the brush.

CHAPTER 3

AGAIN AND AGAIN

S lanted shafts of sunlight reached down between the narrow sides of the ravine. The grass near the edge of the ravine was matted down where something had spent the night. The light fell on Tucker's closed eyelids. The touch of light caused him to slowly open his eyes. As sight came to him so did fear. It was dark, cold, and damp. He lay atop a flat, moss covered rock shelf at the bottom of a steep ravine. Pain overwhelmed his senses. Every part of him ached. Then, the pain was overcome with a sense of foreboding.

"Oh, man," Tucker said looking down at his scratched, scraped, and bloody arms.

His shirt, pants, and socks were torn and wet and caked with blood and mud. He looked up at the nearly vertical inclines on both sides of the ravine.

How am I going to get out of here? I need help. There is no help.

Suddenly he saw his grandparents with their throats cut. Then, he thought of the killers.

I've got to get out of this ravine. If they find me here they'll kill me. Kill me.

He shook with palsy from fear and overexertion the night before. Tears welled in his eyes. He began to sob, and then something happened to him.

It was as if he heard Grandpa Pierce advising him. Grandpa Pierce had a calming tone and reassuring manner when he taught Tucker.

"You're not a child. You're Tucker. Get a hold of yourself.

Remember what Grandpa John taught you. S's. Three S's. Sense. Self. Safe.

Tucker sat up. He began to take stock of his situation. Overcoming his hunger, thirst, and fear he thought hard.

Sense. Take a deep breath and think before you go running off. Well, you didn't do that too well last night. But, you got away. So, take a deep breath now. You got to get out of this hole before they come back. Self. It doesn't look like anything is broken.

Tucker felt his left arm with his right hand, and his right arm with his left hand. He checked his legs and feet.

All right, so you didn't break anything. Thank god for small favors. Okay, pray. You can do that too. You're not getting out of this hole without a little prayer.

I'm thirsty. I'm hungry. Feet are cut. I can't let that get worse. Self.

Tucker ripped his left sleeve from his shirt and tied it around his left foot. He ripped his right sleeve off and tied it around his right foot.

That's better.

Sense. Self. Safe.

Safe. I am not safe down here. I've got to get out of here.

Tucker looked around and up. The ravine was narrow and rock shelves were stacked up on both sides. Dark shadows concealed whatever might be living within this rock structure.

Tucker reached out to a moss covered rock shelf on one side of the ravine and pulled himself up. Looking up to the lightening sky the lip of the ravine seemed a long way up. Tucker guessed it was twenty yards up, but it didn't matter how high it was he had to get out of the ravine. He had to be careful. He couldn't afford to fall down again. He might not be as lucky as he was the first time. He thought of breaking his leg and dying here alone. Then, angry with himself for not concentrating he banished the thought.

Tucker pulled himself up with both hands grasping cold, damp stone. His feet felt for secure places in the rock face. In sequence he reached out with his right hand, then his left hand, and moved his right foot and his left foot. Every muscle in his body ached. Tucker prayed softly that he not get a cramp on his ascent out of the ravine.

No race. Better safe than sorry. Easy does it.

Tucker reached out.

Right hand. Left hand. Right foot. Left foot. Brace.

Not bad. Don't get cocky. Don't overreach. There we go. Probably ten yards. Maybe a third of the way. All right. Reach a little farther this time.

Tucker lost his grip with his right hand, and swung to the left clinging to the rock face with his left hand. The inertia and weight of his body was too much for his left hand to hold. He paid for the mistake by falling back to the bottom. His knee and head struck against rocks. His teeth clattered together. The pain angered him.

"Man!"

Tucker stood up and shook his hands and arms.

"Slow down."

Tucker shook his head.

"Quiet, moron. They could be close."

Looking up Tucker sensed the passage of time with the shift of sunlight.

You got to get out of here. All right. You can do this. You know that. Don't reach too far.

Tucker slowly made his way back up. When he reached the point on the rock face where he fell the first time, he took a deep breath, chose not to look down, and reached not quite as far as he did the last time. He made it. Then he repeated his pattern moving his hands and feet. He looked up and saw the top of the ravine less than ten yards above him.

The end is in sight. Don't look down. Don't move too fast.

Tucker had the sensation that something was watching him. Peering into the darkness at the back of the rock shelf he thought he saw movement. Then, he heard the buzzing sound. Tucker froze. His arms were rigid and still against the rock face. His eyes darted up and around him seeking a path away from this ledge.

His eyes adjusted to the dark revealing a Timber Rattlesnake. Tucker stared motionless at the broad triangular head and dark brown bands across a yellow background. He couldn't see the tail of the snake, but he guessed it was more than three feet long. It was coiled and prepared to strike. He knew what he had to do. The Timber Rattler felt threatened by the sudden arrival of this strange creature before its den. He had unknowingly interrupted the plan of the snake to slither from the cool shadow into the sunlight on the rock shelf and warm itself.

He eased back slowly and the buzzing subsided. As quietly as he could, holding his breath, Tucker moved sideways away from the rattler.

Keep your eyes up. Keep moving.

He finally reached the top ledge, grasped grassy sod and tree roots, and pulled himself over the edge onto the earth. Sweat soaked his hair and his clothes. He breathed deeply. Then, he crawled on all fours a few yards further away from the ravine just to be safe that he did not fall down inside it again. The tracks of his feet were bloody.

"Got to rest, just for a minute," Tucker said leaning back against a tree and falling fast asleep.

CHAPTER 4

ON THE RUN

Tucker listened to the voices. He discerned first one, and then a second, and then a third. The voices were male and older than him.

"Man!"

Tucker shot upright, got to his feet, winced, and darted through the thick brush into the woods. Fear rattled down his spine and made him nauseas. How could he have fallen asleep and let these killers get close to him. They must be behind him at the slope of the ridge leading to the ravine.

"Ow! Man! Man!"

He hobbled painfully through the woods. Each step on a branch or twig caused him more pain. Each thought of those in pursuit spurred him to keep moving.

Dan was the first to the top of the ridge. He knelt at the edge of the ravine. Dan was laughing when the others joined him. He pointed to marks on the wet earth at the edge of the ravine. He glanced at where the grass was matted down, and at the handprints in the earth at the edge of the ravine.

"Kid fell in the ravine. Must be hurt."

He pointed toward the broken brush.

"He can't get far now."

Dan led the others into the woods.

"Blood," Dan said pointing down.

"Let's get him," Jim said.

Rifles at the ready, the three killers moved quickly up the trail left in Tucker's wake.

It was nearly noon now. Broad beams of light broke through the forest canopy. Tucker burst from the woods into a clearing. The thorns of raspberry vines pulled shallow tracks of skin from his forearms. The clearing was filled with ripe raspberries. Hunger pangs rent his stomach, but his concerns were immediately directed to the female brown bear standing on its hind legs in the northern corner of the clearing. He froze with fear at the sight of her, and then the two cubs next to her. He took deep breaths trying to catch his breath.

He wasn't sure she saw him. He was covered in dirt and foliage and blended in with the forest. She was, however, sniffing and searching with her long nose. Behind him, he heard the passage of the killers in pursuit of him. He could not go forward without risking an attack by the bear, and he couldn't go back. He looked to the bear, and then back in the direction of the killers.

Which is better; getting torn to pieces by the bear, or getting shot by the killers?

Tucker stood at the edge of the clearing. His heart pounded in his chest.

He fought hard to remember what Grandpa Pierce had told him. The sounds of his pursuers grew louder. He watched the head of the female brown bear turn toward him.

"Hoorah!" he shouted stepping slowly into the clearing.

He slapped his hands together as loud as he could. The clap echoed in the woods. He had the bear's attention. He shouted as loud as he could. He stretched his body as tall as he could.

"Hoorah! Hoorah!"

The female bear eyed the strange disturbance at the edge of the clearing, and then pushed first one cub and then the other into the woods. They ambled off into the gloom.

Catching a glimpse of his pursuers, Tucker forced himself to sprint across the clearing, enter the woods, and run toward the top of the next ridge. He was dizzy from fatigue and dehydration. He didn't know how much longer he could run, but he could not stop.

CHAPTER 5

AFTER HIM

"Listen," Dan said.

"What in the hell is he doing?" Jim said listening to Tucker's shouts echoing through the woods.

Jim noticed that Dan was slowly turning in a circle as he stared at the woods.

"What?" Jim demanded.

"What do you mean, what?" Dan said.

"What are you doing?"

"Something is watching us. Something's watching us."

Jim shook his head and walked to Dan until his face was inches from Dan's.

"I'm watching you. Now let's move. You two are worse than three year olds. You got the attention span of a dead worm. Something's watching us? You starting to believe those old stories about this valley? Let's move."

Dan continued tracking Tucker. Jim and Mike followed Dan. They stood for a moment on the game trail looking up at the slope of the forested hill in front of them.

"There!" said Mike. "He's near the top."

"You're right. Let's get him."

They saw the boy, obviously in pain, making his way up the game trail.

Exhausted, his upper arms and thighs starting to cramp, cut and bleeding from the branches and thorns grabbing and slapping at him, fear fueled his climb. His feet slipped out from under him and he fell to the ground.

"Quick," said Jim to Dan. "You got him. You got him. Take a shot."

Dan slipped the AK47 off his shoulder, went down on his left knee, and cradled his left elbow against his knee, opened his left hand and rested the rifle stock against it. His heavy breathing caused the front sight blade of the rifle to rise and fall. He fired.

The muzzle blast echoed across the valley putting birds to flight and causing larger animals to freeze and listen. The bullet struck the trunk of a pine several inches away from Tucker's head sending wood splinters tinged with pine sap at him.

"You missed. We got to close the distance."

Jim led the others up the trail. Tucker scrambled up the steep slope on all fours with the men rapidly closing the distance to him.

"All right, all right, we got him now. Take another shot. Can't be more than a hundred yards. You could hit him with a rock at this range."

Dan knelt on one knee. He lined up the front sight blade and the rear sight. The point of aim rose and fell with his breathing as he inhaled and exhaled. He raised the front sight to a spot on the trail just in front of the boy and gently pressed his finger against the trigger taking up the slack. He'd let the boy take another step or two, and then end it.

Tucker looked over his shoulder, his eyes wide with fear, at the men. Tucker felt that his forehead was a large target with a bull's eye on it. Exhausted he waited for the report of the rifle to end his nightmare. He didn't have the strength to move one more inch.

Dan took up the remaining slack in the trigger.

At the top of the ridge, a black silhouette appeared before the blinding yellow sun. The figure stepped into the center of the trail and motioned with its right arm to Tucker.

"Don't," Jim said. "Man, we can't catch a break."

Dan lowered his rifle.

"That's old Grunt. We ain't taking him on out here when he's ready. Let's get out of here. That boy has got more lives than a cat."

"I killed a cat once," Mike said.

"Great," Jim said, pushing Dan and Mike ahead of him down the trail.

Tucker looked at the three men below him who turned and moved away. As they faded from sight moving down the hill Tucker felt his body tremble violently, and then he rolled to his side and vomited.

"Oh God."

Tucker spit to clear the taste from his mouth. The shadow of the tall man fell down across the trail in front of Tucker. The man reached out to Tucker and helped him to his feet.

Tucker saw that the man was tall, and sandy haired with crow's feet under his eyes, and skin weathered from years of exposure to the elements. He looked to Tucker like a picture of a mountain man he'd seen in a history book. The man wore hand-sewn buckskins, and deer skin moccasins; a small leather pouch hung on a cord around his neck, and a water skin with a cork cap was hung over his left shoulder. A wide leather belt was around his waist with a hunting knife in a sheath, and a rifle slung over his shoulder. The man smiled.

CHAPTER 6

AN ALLY

Tucker rubbed his eyes with the bloodied and dirty back of his hand. He stood shaking in front of the man.

"Easy, son. I won't hurt you. You all right? Let me see if you're hurt."

Tucker turned away from this strange man, cradled his head in his hands, and cried.

"I'm not going to hurt you. Show me your face, son. I want to help you. Help me; work with me. You don't seem to have anything broken. What happened to you? Why are you alone?"

The man reached for Tucker. He spun away from him, jumped to his feet, and leaned against a boulder. He looked around as if seeking a rock or a stick; anything he could use as a weapon. The man smiled, and gingerly walked to him.

"They killed my grandma and grandpa. My mom and dad are dead! Everyone's dead. Everyone!"

"I can't bring them back, son. If I could, I would. We got to see to you, now. You got rags on your feet. Look bloody. Got scratches all over you. We got to get you cleaned up and seen to so you don't get an infection. Last thing you want out here is to get an infection."

The man's eyes misted, and he gently laid his hands on Tucker's shoulders. This time Tucker did not turn away. Something deep inside told him he could trust this strange man.

"Go ahead, son, cry. Get it out. I am sorry for all the killing. All of it. You got a friend in me. We'll figure out what to do. Together."

"You promise?"

"That I do. What's your name?"

"Tucker Pierce."

Tucker stared at the man.

"They call me Grunt."

"Grunt? So, you're Grunt?" Tucker said.

Tucker looked over his shoulder down the trail where his pursuers had been.

"And that's why those men were afraid of you?"

"Sounds like you heard of me?"

"Everyone's heard of you. Grandpa…."

Tucker's voice broke at the mention of his grandfather's name and the sudden onslaught of the image of the dead man.

"I'm…"

"It's all right son. I'll take care of you."

Grunt smiled, and took the water skin off his shoulder and offered it to Tucker.

"You must be thirsty."

Tucker hadn't thought of being thirsty, but with the sudden offering he became aware of his dry and parched throat.

"Open your mouth," the man said softly.

Tucker opened his mouth.

"Tilt your head back."

Tucker responded.

The man removed the plug from the water skin, held it several inches over Tucker's mouth, and gently let water fall into the boy's mouth. After a moment he tilted the water skin up.

"More?"

"Please, sir."

Grunt poured a little more water into Tucker's mouth, and then tilted the water skin up, and inserted the wooden plug.

"Careful now, we don't want to make you sick."

The man smiled.

"Can you walk?"

"Yes."

Grunt looked down at the bloody rags on Tucker's feet.

"Sit down against that tree. Let me see what you've done to your feet."

Tucker sat against the trunk of an old pine. Grunt gently untied the shirt sleeves Tucker had wrapped around his feet.

"This may sting a little bit," Grunt said taking the plug out of the water skin. "You ready?"

"I'm ready, sir."

"Somebody taught you well, but you can call me Grunt."

Grunt poured water across the soles of Tucker's feet rinsing away the dirt and blood. Tucker gritted his teeth to keep from crying out from the pain induced by the water into the cuts on his feet. Tucker looked up at Grunt to see if he noticed Tucker's discomfort. He was relieved that he didn't seem to notice.

Grunt removed a pouch from his belt, opened it, and removed a handful of dried plant matter.

"What's that?"

"Sphagnum Moss. Keep you from getting an infection."

Grunt applied the dressing to both of Tucker's feet, and then removed his belt and took off his shirt.

Tucker noticed a dark, black circle just to the left of Grunt's left shoulder. Grunt looked up, and made eye contact with Tucker.

"AK forty seven round went clean through my shoulder. Tore up some flesh but didn't hit the bone."

"AK forty seven? That's the gun that criminals use?"

Grunt laughed.

"I was never a criminal. Before the bad guys used them the North Vietnamese Army used them in Vietnam."

"Vietnam?"

"A long time before you were born."

Grunt used his knife to cut the sleeves from his shirt, wrapped one around each of Tucker's feet to hold the moss dressings in place, and to serve as makeshift moccasins. Placing strain on the index finger of his left hand caused Grunt to wince.

"You all right?" Tucker asked.

"Yeah, I'm fine. Cut my finger a while back. It hasn't healed yet."

"Stand up."

Tucker stood up.

"Take a few steps."

Tucker walked back and forth as if he were in a shoe store trying on new shoes.

"Can you walk okay?"

"Yes, Grunt."

"Good."

Grunt pulled his sleeveless shirt over his head, fastened his belt, and slung his rifle and water skin over his shoulder.

"Okay. Follow me, Tucker Pierce."

"Thank you."

"You're welcome. We got to stick together out here."

Little light fell on Tucker and Grunt as they made their way through the forest on the ancient game trail.

Tucker followed along behind Grunt. Grunt seemed to Tucker to be very much at home in these woods. He hiked along as if he owned the trail. Even the man's clothes seemed to blend in with the other colors of the forest. There was a calm to Grunt that had the same effect on Tucker.

After several hours of hard hiking and pauses for rest Tucker followed Grunt out of the woods into a small clearing before a high ridge.

He trailed Grunt across the clearing to the rock face. Grunt paused at the base of the cliff and then climbed the log ladder and stepped off onto a ledge.

"C'mon up, Tucker."

Tucker's feet hurt as he climbed up the rungs of the wooden ladder. When he reached the top of the ladder, Grunt grasped Tucker's arm and pulled him up.

"You okay?"

"I'll make it."

Grunt smiled.

"I like that."

A tall, wide, log door fit tightly into a wood frame built into the cave's mouth. The man untied a leather knot, and opened the door. He looked toward the woods and nodded as if he were listening.

"What is it?" Tucker asked.

"Just some friends. Those men chasing you are long gone."

Grunt paused.

"At least for now."

Quizzically, Tucker looked back to the woods failing to hear the sound that Grunt had. A blood red sun was setting behind the far hills. Tucker turned back and then stepped inside the cave.

Grunt appeared in the glow of a tallow lamp he held in his hand. Tucker saw that the lamp was made out of a hollowed out stone filled with animal fat. Grunt waved to Tucker to enter.

"Close the door behind you. There's a leather strap to tie it shut."

Grunt turned and started down the passageway.

Tucker closed the door, and tied the strap.

"You don't have to be afraid of me, son," Grunt called out to Tucker.

"I'm not afraid."

"I can see that."

Then, Grunt lit tallow lamps along the wall. Tucker followed along behind moving through shadow and light. The narrow tunnel expanded into a wide, circular chamber. A cot made of logs was in the back. Wool blankets were neatly folded on top of it. A fire pit was in the center of the cave. Rifles, packs, deer skins, and bear skins hung from the wall. A fishing pole made from a slender shaft leaned against the wall. Smoked fish and deer jerky hung from the ceiling. At the apex of the cave, was a small opening to the outside. A few stars flickered. Tucker stood motionless in the chamber.

"Why don't you take yourself a lay down while I get some grub rustled up?"

"I'm not hungry."

The man looked over his shoulder at Tucker, and then placed firewood onto the smoldering coals. The dry wood quickly burst into flames.

"Been in the woods much?"

Tucker buried his head in his hands and sobbed heavily. He was embarrassed in front of this stranger, but he couldn't help himself.

"Well, Tucker, you got yourself dealt one God-awful deal. No two ways about it. Like I said, I am truly sorry about your family. I ain't heard about something like that since..."

Tucker looked up.

"Since when?"

"It don't matter. What matters now is you. Let me get you some food."

"I'm not hungry."

The man's voice took on a sternly paternal tone to Tucker.

"How long you been in the woods, boy?"

Tucker spoke through his tears. His voice broke.

"My Grandpa and Grandma Pierce been taking me since I was six."

"Pierce? Grandpa Pierce? John Pierce?"

"Yes. Did you know him?"

"Know of him, part time game warden. Decent man. How old you now? Thirteen, fourteen?"

"Fifteen."

"All that time in the woods. What did your Grandpa teach you about survival?"

"Eat when you can, 'cause you don't know when you're gonna' eat next, and don't waste anything."

"He taught you well. Besides, can't think right if you're hungry. You take a rest, and I'll get us some food. Have some hot Beechnut coffee in a few minutes. It's probably time you started drinking coffee."

The man opened a tin can, scooped out a pale, brown paste with his fingers, and worked the paste into the shape of thin pancakes.

Tucker watched and then looked around the cave. For a minute he thought maybe he was still at the bottom of the ravine imagining all of this.

"What's that?"

"Pancakes, you like pancakes, don't you?"

"You got pancake mix out here?"

"My own making. You take acorns, boil'em up for a couple of hours, gets rid of the bitterness, then pour off the water, soak the nuts in cold water for four days, 'course you got to change the water each day, and then grind them into a paste, and you got pancake batter."

Tucker wiped the tears from his eyes.

"Okay."

The man poured two cups of coffee, and dropped in two pinches of sugar from a tin canister. He placed the cups on the stones around the fire, scooped up two pancakes from the skillet, and handed an aluminum plate, with a fork inside it, and a cup to Tucker.

"Thank you."

"You are welcome, sir."

"It's all right, Tucker. Go on and eat."

They ate quickly and silently. The taste of food after a night and day without any sparked Tucker's appetite. He barely chewed the food as he swallowed it.

Before Tucker finished his meal the combined effect of safety, warmth, and shelter overwhelmed him. Two of the three S's thought Tucker as he fell asleep.

Grunt caught Tucker's plate before it could hit the cave floor. Grunt covered Tucker with a blanket, and then wrapped himself in a blanket, and added logs to the fire.

"Get a good sleep, young trooper."

Grunt rustled in a pack on the floor and took out a neatly folded buckskin shirt and pants. Feeling in the dim light he found a small bag and took it. He glanced up to see that Tucker was sound asleep. He put the small bag and buckskin shirt and pants under his right arm.

A blanket wrapped around him, and carrying an aluminum coffee cup in his good hand, Grunt made his way back up the passageway, untied the door, and stepped out on the cave ledge.

Hundreds of faint, blue, translucent fires dotted the forest floor below and the ridges surrounding the valley. Shimmering shapes moved around the fires.

Grunt rubbed his bandaged finger, its putrid stench worrisome. He winced, smiling weakly.

"Been seeing a lot more of you boys lately. Some kind of omen."

For a moment, Grunt thought he caught sight of a pair of red eyes at the edge of the clearing. He shook his head. He had seen so many strange sights in this valley this was just one more.

Grunt set his coffee cup down on the cold stone rock face. Opening the bag he took out a scissors, a needle, and thread.

Grunt looked up at the Milky Way from time to time as he worked. On occasion his right hand holding the needle touched his left hand. The pain from his index finger traveled up his arm like a shock. Grunt continued working until he was done, finished his coffee, and then went back inside the cave to check on his guest.

CHAPTER 7

DREAMS

Tucker slept fitfully in the strange surroundings. His dreams came as rapidly as his breathing. His feet twitched as if he were still running through the forest.

In his dream Amanda wore John's green faded jungle hat, a much washed pastel yellow sweatshirt, Levis, and hiking boots. The nearby stream coursed through the dark, thickly forested valley. Her straw colored hair had a gold hue in the late afternoon sunlight, and was tucked under a New Chatham Tigers' baseball cap. Feeble rays of twilight hid the rows of lines beneath her eyes. She sat on a small, weathered gray boulder next to Tucker.

John Pierce wore a heavily stained, faded baseball cap, a black and red mackinaw, Levis, and boots. His tall form was painted half in shadow and half in sunlight. His attention was directed to three packets of freeze dried meals immersed in a pot of boiling water.

"What are you thinking about, Grandma?" Tucker asked.

"Oh, I was just thinking how much I love your Grandpa."

Tucker laughed.

"That's a no brainer, Grandma. Everyone in town knows that."

"Yes," Amanda said, "I guess they do at that."

She smiled.

"Not much of a secret."

Tucker looked over the yellow glow of the crackling campfire surrounded by a ring of stones. The smoke from the campfire rose and mingled with the mist coming from the stream.

"I love it up here, Grandma. It's so different than the city. There's so much more stuff that nature made than people made."

Tucker looked off across the stream at the dark wall of pine trees on the far bank.

"What's over there, Grandpa?"

"Don't know," John Pierce answered. "Never been in this deep before. If you want, we can check it out in the morning."

Amanda put her arm around Tucker and smiled.

"I remember when we first took you camping. When you were little. You were afraid to come here. You used to say you saw things here."

"I remember," Tucker said. "It was bears. I was afraid of bears."

He laughed.

"I was little then. But, I still saw things."

"Like what?" Amanda asked.

"It's like the Indians are still here, and sometimes soldiers. You can't see them if you look right at them. But, sometimes they just sort of appear."

"You've got a real imagination."

The snap of a branch breaking echoed from the dark woods at the edge of the campsite.

"Maybe that's one of them," Tucker said.

He rose, stepping between Amanda and the fire, raising his arms to his side.

"Could've been right here. Hundreds of years ago. A war party of Algonquians…"

"How about a hunting party?"

"Okay, but war party would have been cooler…"

John glanced up from the frying pan at the sound of Tucker pronouncing the word "war."

"…hunting party," Tucker continued. "Maybe ten, twelve, camping for the night. Maybe fishing like us."

He grinned.

"Sitting right there. Maybe our fire is on top of theirs. Maybe we ought to dig around here. See if there's arrowheads and stuff. Maybe bone."

"Some things best left buried, Tuck," John said.

"So," Amanda said, "your hunting party. What happens next?"

Tucker rubbed his chin, looked over his shoulder at the stream, and then turned back to Amanda. "They cross the stream…" Tucker grinned broadly "…and they get ambushed by a Mohawk <u>war party</u>."

He laughed.

"Enough of war parties for tonight, Tucker," Amanda said.

"I'm going to be a soldier when I grow up."

"You are, huh?"

Amanda looked long and steady at Tucker, and then at John.

"You have a long time before you have to think about that, Tucker."

"Oh, I know, Grandma. I can enlist at eighteen; that's only three years away."

John shook his head.

"You don't know what it means to be a soldier in war."

"You do."

"Yes. Don't be so anxious to get there. What do you say we enjoy the woods. I got some more field skills I can teach you tomorrow."

"Grandpa's the best woodsman ever was."

John looked to the wall of tall pines. His face grew solemn.

"I'm good, but there's one better than me."

His eyebrows arched as he spoke.

The thick woods ran down to the edge of the river and up to the crests of the surrounding hills. The wind tossed the tops of the tall pines adding its voice to that of the white water stream flashing in contrast to the deepening night.

"There's one out here," John continued, "that gives old Jim Bridger a run for his money. I'm good, but not as good as Grunt."

"You never told me about Grunt before, Grandpa," Tucker said.

"Didn't want to scare you, Tucker, when you were little. Some folks in town make him out to be like a boogey man. He isn't. Word is he was a soldier, a real warrior."

"Tell me, please."

"Well, he's been out here so long he's part of the woods. He knows the woods; the creatures out here know him. Lucky devil, survive that long alone. Least ways, we think he's alone. Came back from war..."

John looked out at the forest.

"Sort of created his own world out here. Leave the war and folks behind. Lord, there are all sorts of rumors about him and Indian spirits out here, but I've never seen any. He's a woodsman. Every now and again, some hunter claims he's seen him. Only see Grunt when he wants to be seen. Every few months, he walks into town, wearing his best buckskins; goes over to Buck's; gets some ammo, then drops into the library and gets some books."

John shook his head.

"Think about that Tuck. Got to carry ammo, whatever other supplies he needed and books, too. No, Tucker, I'm good, but he's the best there is. Well, let's call it a night."

John rolled out three worn, and faded sleeping bags a discreet distance from the low fire.

"I'm going to explore before it gets dark."

John reached into his pack, removed two small two-way radios, handed one to Tucker, and turned the other one on, placing it near him.

"Radio check," John spoke into the radio.

"Base Camp, this is Tucker, over."

"Base Camp, Roger," John said. "Keep in sight of the fire, and head back before nightfall."

"I'll be careful, Grandpa. I just want to look around. This is a cool place."

"I know you will. I trained you."

Tucker strolled off in the twilight toward the stream. An orange shard of the sun was slipping behind a hilltop. The rumbling rush of the stream reverberated within the thick, dark pines. Overhead, bats appeared as darting, black dots against the deep gray clouds. Tucker breathed in the sharp pine scent feeling intensely alive as it filled his lungs. The rich, loamy air was intoxicating. Tucker bent down by the edge of the sparkling, clear mountain water, plucked cool wet stones from the bank, and tossed them into the water. Some clicked against streambed rocks while others made a solitary splash before sinking to the bottom. He tapped two stones together making a clicking sound.

"Snipes." Tucker laughed, remembering his first Snipe hunt with Grandpa.

"Snipes."

He laughed again, hitting another boulder. He remembered the sharp click of two rocks, and then the weight in his rucksack of another snipe. The love between Tucker and his grandfather was deep. Somehow, even though Grandpa was in charge, Tucker considered himself to be his equal. He knew Grandma and Grandpa were authority figures like his mother and father, but their way was different.

Watching a lumbering gray cloud alter in the winds aloft, for an instant he was a naval captain guiding a great sailing ship across a tangerine sea. Standing on the bridge of his flagship, HMS Defiant, Tucker signaled his flotilla to maneuver. Dozens of ships of the line sailed in two parallel columns. There, on the distant horizon, Captain Tucker saw the enemy fleet attempting to escape.

"Onward, men; we'll catch them. More sail! More speed!"

Captain Tucker gave the order when they were within range. Gun ports opened; cannons were hoisted forward; and the cannonade commenced. Puffs of gray smoke blossomed along the ships as cannons barked and recoiled.

"Avast, me hearties," Tucker said, laughing at his own humor. "Avast, me hearties? What does that mean?"

A lone black bat swooped low, racing mere inches above the stream, catching the members of the rising hatch of insects. The bat sped toward Tucker like a barnstormer barely missing him, and then soared into the gathering darkness. His eyes caught the bat and followed it into the darkening sky.

For a moment, Tucker was a young Royal Air Force lieutenant.

"Left-tenant," Tucker said, enjoying the sound of the word, and strapping himself into a pale, green Spitfire. Evening dew caused the grass airfield to glisten. Flashing a 'thumbs up' to his ground crew, Tucker pushed the throttle forward, taxiing down the field. Lifting into the air with other 'Spits' on his right and left, Tucker looked high above to the bright blue field of battle. Soaring through the cold sky, Tucker spotted the 'Jerries'. ME109s. Diving, guns spitting fire, Tucker dove through the ME109s shooting down two in his first pass. He returned to a hero's welcome at the field, and enjoyed a brief respite and a cup of tea on a couch on the grass airfield before the next aerial combat.

He ambled down the streambed glancing over his shoulder from time to time to make sure he could still see the fire. The roar of the rushing water filled his ears. His eyes tried hard to pierce the falling veil of night as he casually strolled over rocks and around pools of swirling water. He stopped abruptly, swinging around as if in response to hearing his name.

"There's no one here."

Tucker's heart pumped rapidly ready to provide fresh blood for fight or escape.

"There's no one here," Tucker said louder, trying to convince himself.

"Don't go crazy. Grandpa said the woods play tricks on you. This is just a trick."

Tucker clenched the two-way radio in his left hand. *No, only a baby would call for help. You're not a baby. There's nothing here. Sounds like my name. No, just the wind. The roar of the water, that's all.*

Tucker slowly turned in a circle staring into the woods.

Look a little off center, way to see at night, said Grandpa. Can't look straight ahead in the night. Cones or rods or something.

Sweat from fear pooled beneath Tucker's arms and on his back.

The woods began to appear as a single dark wall. Tucker could no longer make out the individual pines. A pin-point of flickering yellow light contrasted sharply with the night. Hesitatingly, as if being drawn away from a discovery, he walked slowly back to camp.

I know.

Tucker stretched out his right arm before his head to feel with his hand for unseen branches.

It's a game. Some kind of hide and seek. The brave explorer comes too close and something leads him away.

The campfire ahead steadily grew in size and intensity as Tucker neared it. Pausing, looking back over his shoulder, he thought he could see a pale, faint blue light without shape. It seemed to flicker as a burning fire. Staring harder, he thought he could see several shapes near the strange fire, but he couldn't make them out. He shook his head, closed and opened his eyes, and whatever it might have been was gone.

He stepped into the fire's circle of light. Seeing him, John turned off the two-way radio next to him.

"Cut it close, Tuck."

"Grandpa…"

Tucker looked back at the woods, then back to John.

"Do you…nothing."

"What is it, Tuck?"

"Nothing."

Tucker sat down on his sleeping bag, removed his hiking shoes, then his shirt and pants, and placed them inside his pack. Feet first, he slipped into the sleeping bag pulling it tight around his chest. His body quickly fit itself to the comforting contours of the thin pad beneath him. Amanda leaned over and kissed him on the forehead.

"Good night, young man."

"Good night, Grandma. Good night, Grandpa."

"'Night, Tuck."

Tucker listened to the roar of the stream, felt the touch of wind, and stared in awe at the sight above him. Uncountable, brilliant white pin-points of light filled the black background of night.

Tucker tossed fitfully. The cocoon of the sleeping bag clammy with his sweat seemed to fight him as he sought comfort. Face to the cot, face to the ceiling, face buried under the sleeping bag, no matter how he arranged his aching body, he could not shutter from his mind the unwelcome images. He was no longer camped on the river bank with his grandparents. He was floating in space.

Ann, Tucker's mother, a comely woman in her early forties wearing her favorite green print dress, waved to Tucker as she disappeared into darkness. Tucker tried to call out to her, but his throat was sealed. Steven, Tucker's father and best friend, flailed his arms struggling to reach Tucker. Tucker reached out for him, but Steven disappeared into darkness leaving Tucker completely alone.

Tucker shuddered, and then he awoke. Images flashed before him of Grandpa John and Grandma Amanda's throats red with blood. He was running through the brush with it slapping at him in return. Only a few feet before him on the ledge in the ravine the Timber Rattlesnake slowly raised its wedge shaped head buzzing at him. Then, atop the ridge the black shape appeared against the rising yellow sun.

Tucker shivered. Looking over at the long dark shape on the cave floor he eyed Grunt, and resolved not to wake the stranger who had befriended him. Here he was crying at night like a child. He wasn't a child. Not anymore. And then, the deep melancholia overwhelmed his false bravado.

Everything was gone. Everything was changed. There was no way back to his old life, and he could not see a way ahead. For the first time in his life, Tucker was painfully conscious of himself, his mortality, and the unpredictable and violent world in which he lived. If his parents could be killed in a car crash, and if murderers could take the lives of his grandparents, what safety was there in this world?

CHAPTER 8
A PARTNERSHIP

T ucker noticed that Grunt was awake.

"I'm sorry, I didn't mean to wake you up."

"Not a problem. Can't sleep?" Grunt propped himself up on one elbow.

"Bad dream."

"Had me a few."

Grunt rolled to his side and rose from the cot.

"C'mon, let's get some starlight. It's good for the soul. Sit up for a while maybe you'll sleep better."

Tucker pulled back the sleeping bag. His polo shirt and jeans were in tatters.

"Here," Grunt said.

He handed Tucker a cut down buckskin shirt and pants. "Try these."

Tucker looked at his shirt, and then at the buckskins he took from Grunt.

"Thanks."

Grunt went down the narrow passageway to the mouth of the cave. Once Tucker had changed into the buckskins he followed Grunt and stepped out into the cool night air. A breeze plucked droplets of sweat from the back of Tucker's neck.

"Not bad," Grunt said.

He eyed his sewing job.

"I guessed your height."

Grunt sat on one of the three stones around the fire pit.

"Here, try these on. We'll check your bandages in the morning."

Grunt handed Tucker a pair of moccasins that he had altered to fit Tucker's feet.

"Thank you."

Tucker sat on one of the stones by the fire pit and gently eased his feet into the moccasins.

"If they're loose you can tighten up those cords that run around the outside.

"They're fine, Grunt. Thanks."

Above them the Milky Way shone as piercing, uncountable pin pricks of light scattered within a wide waving band across the night sky.

"I'm sorry about that."

Tucker nodded toward the cave.

"What?"

"Bad dream. You know…"

Grunt smiled. "It don't matter, Tucker."

Grunt looked up at the sparkling stars.

"Anybody who's lived a bit will have those from time to time. No shame in that."

Grunt looked into Tucker's eyes.

"I've had my share. I tell you that. What was yours about?"

"A year ago," Tucker said softly. "My mother, and father, and me, we'd just had dinner with my grandparents. In the summer I spend a week or two with them. And my dad and mom had driven up to pick me up."

Tucker looked away from Grunt as if he could see images of his words in the distance. He knew the images would bring tears and he did not want to cry in front of Grunt.

"We were just at the edge of town. I was in the back seat. I didn't see anything, but somebody hit us. We went off the road."

Tears welled in Tucker's eyes.

"My mom and dad were hurt real bad. They died in the hospital. When I woke up my Grandma Amanda and Grandpa John were there."

"Horrible accident."

"Maybe. There was rust and paint on the front fender where somebody hit us."

Tucker's voice revealed his anger.

"Somebody hit us and drove off! My whole family is lying hurt on the ground and they drive off! And, they stole my dad's wallet and mom's purse. Who would do something like that?"

"Some kind of scum," Grunt said. "You could have been hit by a drunk. Then he runs off not to get caught. But stealing from hurt folks? That's pretty low. I ain't never heard of that before."

"Someday," Tucker said with great resolve. "I'll find them."

"So, that was your nightmare?"

"I'm sorry…"

"Don't be. You've been through a lot."

"What's going to happen to me?"

"We don't have to figure that out tonight."

"You have nightmares?"

Grunt smiled and took a deep breath.

"Oh, not as often as they were once. I've had my share of beauts I'll tell you that."

Grunt chuckled.

"I had this one, one night. I dreamed that these giant frogs as big as a small cottage were outside. They had pith helmets with red stars on them, and carried AK forty sevens. They were taunting me to come out."

Grunt whistled.

"Scared the devil out of me."

"You? Scared?"

"What? Everybody gets scared sometimes."

"Yeah, but a guy…"

"A guy? Guys don't cry and don't get scared?"

Grunt smiled.

"Sort of."

"It's not that you don't get scared, it's that you don't run from it."

"What if other people think that…"

"It don't matter," Grunt said interrupting Tucker.

"You say that a lot."

"Hmm?"

"It don't matter."

"It don't matter. Don't mean nothing. That's what we used to say in my war."

"You had your own war?"

Tucker looked at Grunt.

Grunt smiled.

"You know, I never thought about it that way, until just now when you asked the question. But, I guess I did have my own war. All soldiers do. They bring it home with them. Most of them have it locked up in a chest in the back of their minds, and then sometimes a nightmare pops the lid and escapes until they can put it back in."

"I'm gonna' be a soldier."

"You are, are you?"

"After I track down who killed my parents. I'm going to enlist and go kill terrorists."

"You best think long and hard on that before you sign up."

"You went."

"That's why I said what I said. You could end up in a place like this."

Grunt looked out at the valley.

"What is this place?" Tucker asked. "My grand…we never came in this far before."

"This place?"

Grunt nodded at the dots of pale blue light across the valley floor.

"The Indians lived in this valley thousands of years before the White Man came. Once he came, then it all changed for the Indians and for the valley. Really changed with the revolution."

"How?"

"You read about it in school?"

"Boston Tea Party. Shots at Concord Bridge."

"Well, I bet your history books didn't teach you about this valley. During the American Revolution the Indian nation split on whom to back. Some wanted to fight for the British, some for the colonists. Some saw the White Man's war as an economic opportunity. Some saw the war bringing great danger. Seventeen seventy eight, the colonists attacked. Wyoming Massacre, Cherry Valley Raid, Battle of Oriskany. General John Sullivan, and a host of his friends attacked trying to kill all the Indians. They didn't. Some survivors made it back to this valley choosing it to perform rituals called Manitou's. From the ceremony, came visions, and in the visions supernatural beings talked to them."

Grunt paused, looked to Tucker, and then looked out at the valley.

"Some say those spirits remain in this valley to this day and are open to those who seek them, and are deadly to those who offend them. Some say it's because of those spirits that some strange things happen in here."

"How come nobody put a farm in here?"

"Oh they tried way back when. Two handled logging saws turned red hot when the blades were put to Old Growth trees. The first loggers saw strange things during the day and heard stranger sounds at night which frightened them from the valley. No hunters, fishers, trappers, and campers come here."

"We did."

Tucker took a deep breath with the image of his dead grandparents on his mind.

"If only..."

"Don't go there."

"But..."

"There's no but. It happened. It's done. Now, we got to figure out what we're going to do with you."

"You think those men are after me?"

"They won't give up. I know of them. They're no good."

Grunt picked up a few pebbles from the cliff and swirled them around in his fingers like worry beads.

"Those three are the scum of the earth."

"Why were they afraid of you?"

"Were they?"

Grunt smiled.

"They turned away when you showed up. They sure seemed scared to me."

"Some folks think I'm crazy."

"Are you?"

"How would I know? Do I look like I'm crazy to you?"

"What does crazy look like?"

Grunt laughed softly.

"Think you can sleep now?"

Tucker nodded.

CHAPTER 9
WHICH IS BETTER

Outside the cave White-tailed Deer appeared; dark brown shapes in contrast to the pale, gray background of the heavy fog. Gracefully, the deer stepped around the trunks of tall, dark pines. A pair of Red Tailed hawks circled in convection currents above the valley as the sun crested the trees, and the birds looked down for prey.

Sunlight crawled down the tall trees across the clearing, and then up the ridge toward Grunt's cave. Fingers of light pierced the thin gap below the rough-hewn, log cave door. Grunt sat up and leaned back against the cave wall, stretching his arms, and rubbing his face. His bare legs were dotted with faint, purple scars from shrapnel. Unconsciously, Grunt rubbed the scar on his shoulder as if the physical pain were still present. He scratched his chest revealing two scars each one dead center over each lung.

⊨╫╫⊨

In an instant he was there. Baking hot jungle. Bullets whizzing like bees past his ears. Grunt flat on his back with others tending to him.

He was dizzy and confused looking up to the faces of others hovering above him. His arms and legs were held down by soldiers. Nearly unconscious watching Truth shouting at the others while he kept both his palms on Grunt's chest. Out of the corner of his eyes he saw others in his squad pull cigarette packs out of their pockets and toss them to Truth. Truth took the cellophane from one pack, held it between his teeth, and nodded to a soldier. Truth removed his hands from the puncture wounds in Grunt's lungs, then placed one cellophane wrapper over the wound and taped it. He did the same with the other wound. By sealing the wounds to Grunt's lungs Truth had saved his friend's life.

⊷⊶

And then, Grunt was back. Sunlight coming through the opening in the cave roof provided faint light inside the cave. It was a coincidence of nature that at this time of year the rising sun cast its light down the passageway.

"Morning, Grunt," Grunt said.

He looked to his right.

"Good morning, Grunt," Grunt said.

He looked to his left.

"Another day in paradise."

Tucker opened his eyes, was startled by his surroundings until he remembered where he was, and whom he was with. He sat up on the cot, and rubbed his eyes. He recognized Grunt, and the cave.

"You always say good morning to yourself?"

"Since I been out here, you the first what's been in my cave. I talk to myself to remember how to talk. When I first came out here I was in the woods for almost a month before I went back into town. My throat didn't work right, and I couldn't seem to find words."

"What are those scars?"

"What?"

"Those scars."

Tucker pointed at Grunt.

"Oh. You saw the AK scar when we met. These others? Grenade fragments."

Grunt took a deep breath. He looked at Tucker, looked at the scars, and then back to Tucker.

"I was a soldier once. Long time ago."

"Tell me about the war. Did you kill a lot of people?"

"You never ask a soldier that."

"Why?"

"It's not polite. Besides, just look at him. You'll tell."

"How?"

"His eyes when you ask. You'll see hesitation. He may squint his eyes a bit as if he's looking off in the distance. He wants to tell you something. But, he knows if you aren't a warrior, he can't tell you. No way to get from where he's been to what you want to know."

Grunt cleared his throat.

"We got some good daylight, decent day. What say we get some groceries?"

"Groceries? You don't want to talk about the war, do you?"

"You're a smart kid."

Grunt rose to his feet towering over Tucker.

"I would dearly love to answer your questions, son, but some things I can't tell you. I mean, I could tell you, but you wouldn't understand."

"Why?"

"Just haven't lived enough, son."

"That's not my fault."

"No, it's not your fault."

Grunt paused.

"And don't be in too much of a rush to get older."

"Why do they call you Grunt?"

"That's what they called infantry in my war C'mon."

Grunt led the way out of the cave to the fire pit on the ledge. Grunt placed a layer of kindling wood on the coals of last night's fire. He exhaled a deep breath blowing the gray powder from the coals.

They glowed red for moment, caused the kindling to smolder, and then catch fire.

Grunt stoked the fire and placed a dented faded blue coffee pot on a metal grid over the fire.

"This will put hair on your chest."

Grunt nodded at the coffee pot. Soon, the brackish, brown liquid resonated within the stained glass cap on the top of the percolator.

"Last night's coffee. Don't waste a thing out here."

"I bet that's going to taste good," Tucker said. "No, I'm sorry I didn't mean that. I didn't mean to sound smart."

Grunt shook a tin container.

"Secret is sugar. Put enough sugar on it you can eat almost anything."

"So, let me understand this. You live out here all alone. You talk to yourself so you don't forget how to talk?"

Grunt picked up a tin cup, opened the tin and removed a sugar cube, dropped it into the cup, and then filled it with Beechnut coffee and handed it to Tucker.

"Careful, it's hot."

Grunt filled a second cup and quickly sipped from it.

"Ah, that's powerful."

Tucker sipped the hot coffee.

"Oh, that's powerful all right."

They both laughed.

"I talk to others."

"Others? I thought you were alone out here?"

"People wise that is. I talk to the deer. The wolves."

Grunt turned away from Tucker. Looking back at Tucker, Grunt winked.

Tucker sipped his coffee. "You talk to wolves?"

"Every damn day. They tell me lots of things."

Tucker laughed heartily. "Like what? What can a wolf tell you?"

"What can a wolf tell me? Think about it. He's got a better sense of smell, five hundred, five thousand times better. Better hearing. Better eyesight. He can move quiet and soft and sneak right up on you, and…he's been roamin' around these mountains for thousands of years."

"Not the same one."

"How do we know?"

Grunt grinned.

"Could be. Lot of things I don't know for sure, and a lot of things I don't know at all."

Grunt sipped his coffee. "I tell you what's really smart out here are the coy dogs."

"Coy dogs?"

"Yeah, coy dogs. Offspring of coyotes and dogs. They've got all the cleverness of the coyote, and all the steadfast qualities of dogs. I've run into them once or twice."

Grunt handed Tucker several pieces of venison jerky. Tucker clutched the hard, thin strips in his right hand.

"How come you got three seats here if no one has ever visited you?" Tucker asked.

"Maybe I knew you was coming."

Grunt laughed.

"Truth is, those stone seats was here when I got here. Probably dragged out here by whoever lived in the cave before me. We're just passing through, son. Everything in this valley is recyclable. Those tall pines, maybe last a hundred years, come crashing down in a storm, rot, then all them seeds they been dropping on the forest floor spring up. Start it all over. It just keeps going until the end."

"The end? What is the end?"

"A little philosophy here in the morning? Depends on what you believe. 'Course you got to start with the beginning."

"What was the beginning?"

"You got a faith?"

"I suppose. I went to Sunday school. I believe in Jesus, and God, and angels."

"Then," Grunt said sipping the still warm Beechnut coffee, "you got your beginning. 'In the beginning, God created the heavens and earth. The earth was without form and void, and darkness was upon the face of the deep; and the Spirit of God was moving over the face of the waters.' That's all right for a beginning."

"What's your beginning?

"Not exactly sure. I like That Which Rested On The Back of the Four Tortoises."

"I don't get it."

"Indian religion. Had their own way of looking at things."

"Which is better?"

Grunt laughed.

"If you or me could answer that…All comes down to faith."

Tucker turned away from Grunt and stared into the woods below. The now familiar deep melancholia came over him without warning. His throat constricted until he felt as if he couldn't breathe. The horrid images of his grandparents came to him. The odor of the hospital room came back to him. He remembered the looks on his grandparents' faces and knew that his parents were gone. Tears washed down his cheeks. His chest heaved as he sobbed. Tucker felt Grunt's hand on his right shoulder.

Tucker looked up crying. Grunt smiled weakly and nodded.

"It's going to be all right, son. I promise."

The sun had risen above the trees casting shadows across the clearing. Spiracles of mist rose from the forest floor and ascended above the treetops. Great clouds of mist moved along the valley slopes as a tide. Dew glistened on the tall, brown grass in the meadow.

A moose limped from the woods, paused warily at the tree line, and then ambled into the clearing.

Tucker's crying gradually subsided. Tucker wiped his tears on his sleeve.

"That's old Two Step," Grunt said.

He pointed down at a large, old moose entering the clearing.

"Two Step? Two Step the moose?"

"Two Step's been comin' by for years. Gettin'older, limpin' now. Lost his harem years ago. He's an outcast like me."

"You're not an outcast. I need you."

"You need me all right. You can't survive out here without me. That's dangerous. Something happens to me, it's over for you. We got to figure out what to do with you."

"Teach me."

"You've got to go back you know. You've got to tell them about your grandparents. How long were you going to be out? I mean your grandpa must have told someone in town when you'd be coming out?"

"A week. We were going to be out for a week."

"You got to go back."

"I don't want to."

Grunt's eyes steeled over.

"Life ain't about what you want. It's about what you are. That's all there is, son. And what you are is a member of a family."

"I don't have a family. Everyone is dead. My mother, my father, my grandma and grandpa."

Tucker, crying, turned away from Grunt. His shoulders shook.

"You must have other family, aunts, uncles, friends, school?"

"I hate them. They're not nice. I don't have a family."

"You're talking like a child."

"I am a child."

Grunt knelt before Tucker and placed his hands on his shoulders. "No, not anymore, young trooper. You're a <u>man</u> who needs need help, and we're gonna' do what's right."

"What do you mean?"

"Okay, you spend a few days with me, here in the woods, if you want. I don't see any harm in that. In a way it's a tribute to your Grandpa John. He started out teaching you about the woods. I'll finish it."

Grunt looked at Tucker.

"Then, you got to go back. Pact?"

"Okay," Tucker said extending his hand. "A pact."

Grunt accepted Tucker's hand and shook it hard

"Okay, finish our coffee, and we'll get started. Daylight's a wasting."

As Grunt and Tucker sat on the ledge sipping coffee and looking out on the clearing an unseen animal at the edge of the woods made a furrow in the brush as she paced back and forth like an impatient pup waiting for her master to take her outside.

"What's that, at the edge of the woods? Something's there, but I can't see it?" Tucker asked.

Grunt smiled.

"There's a lot in this valley you can't see unless they want you to. Keep your heart open the next few days; you'll see a lot."

"You don't see with your heart."

"Out here you do. Out here it ain't thinking that keeps you alive. It's watching, and listening, and knowing. Knowing the normal sounds and smells and feelings, and then noticing what's not. It's the what's not normal out here that'll get you. Finish your coffee. Let's get going and we'll give you your first lesson in staying alive out here."

CHAPTER 10

VO XU

Tucker watched Grunt put his arms through a small knapsack, and then slip the canvas strap of his rifle over his shoulder.

"You ready?"

"Yeah."

Tucker followed Grunt down the ladder on the side of the cliff, across the small clearing, and into the dark woods. They walked along in silence through the thick forest.

Tucker looked up at the breaks in the tree cover where sunlight came through. He listened to the rustle of wind through the leaves making a sound like gentle surf. He listened to the call of birds. He recognized the call of crows, but there were other birds here he did not know.

He looked at his buckskins. He clutched them with his right hand, and smiled, and then looked ahead at Grunt. He felt a new sense of pride. He felt a connection to Grunt.

"Old game trail."

Grunt pointed down.

Tucker nodded and smiled. The cool early morning dew made the packed earth of the game trail slick beneath their feet and they left long diagonal tracks on the surface slipping as they walked. Every so often, each of them had to reach out, grasp the trunk of a nearby tree, and hold it to keep from falling. The trees and foliage came right to the edges of the narrow path.

"We rest here for five," Grunt said.

Grunt sat on the ground with his back to a tall oak. Tucker nodded, and sat next to him.

He watched Grunt stare at the gently swaying underbrush lining the game path. The underbrush on both sides of the trail was as a door opening and closing in the wind. Grunt seemed hypnotized by the motion. Tucker watched as Grunt's eyes closed and his facial features grew taut. For a moment, Tucker was afraid that Grunt might go into a trance and not wake up. Several moments passed before Grunt looked at Tucker.

"Where were you?"

Tucker looked around the forest, and then back to Grunt.

Grunt smiled.

"In a place I hope you never go. C'mon; the pond is just up ahead."

Tucker shook his head, thought of asking a question, but then decided that if Grunt wanted to tell him something he would.

Grunt and Tucker stood before a small pond filled with cattails. The brown cylindrical heads of the plants swayed back and forth in the breeze. The pond, the size of a football field, was nestled against the face of a ridge. A small stream fed it at one end, and a beaver dam at the other regulated its depth. Water bugs skated across its surface.

"First stop."

Grunt knelt, and with one smooth pull removed a long hunting knife from his belt.

"Good crop of cattails in there."

Grunt cut six cattails down, then cut the rootstalks and rinsed them in the water. He placed the stalks in a worn, leather sack slung over his shoulder.

"Just like asparagus if you cook them up right. Let's go."

Grunt rose, slapped at mud on his knees, and led Tucker further into the woods.

"Here we are."

Grunt knelt by a patch of reddish flowers, dug into the soil, and plucked the bulbs of wild onions. He placed those in his bag.

"Cook us up a stew tonight."

"Time for a little flour."

"Flour?"

Tucker looked around as if seeking a grocery store. "I don't…"

"C'mon, I'll show you."

Grunt drew his blade down the trunk of a young pine, stripped the outer bark away, and then cut pieces of the inner bark from the tree, and placed them in his pack.

"Dry her out and grind it down into flour. Got vitamin C in it."

"I want to learn everything you can teach me," Tucker said.

He turned in a circle.

"I didn't know. I mean I know the Indians lived off the land, but I never knew that normal people did."

"Are you listening to yourself?" Grunt said with a smile. "Indians aren't normal, and I am?"

Grunt scratched the top of his head.

"A lot of people would say you got that just about backwards."

"I meant…

"Just kidding you. If you really think about it, it wasn't that long ago that we all lived like this."

Tucker followed Grunt up the trail.

"Got one!"

Grunt stepped several feet into the underbrush on the side of the trail. A small game trail joined the main trail. Grunt leaned over a rope noose which had snared a rabbit. The fat brown rabbit swung by the neck in the noose. Its glazed eyes bulged. Grunt took the animal in his hands, and removed it from the noose. He made a cut behind the head large enough for his fingers, and then peeled the skin backwards. He gutted the animal. He dipped the rabbit carcass in the nearby stream, rinsed it, and then wrapped it in fresh green leaves and dropped it in his sack.

"There we go. Little rabbit stew for dinner. Rabbit, cattail asparagus, and onions. So, you like it out here?"

Tucker nodded.

A low growl came from the nearby woods. Grunt took his rifle off his shoulder, and raised it.

"Stay behind me, son."

"What is it?"

"Don't rightly know. Whatever it is, it's close, and wants to let us know it's here."

Tucker stepped behind Grunt.

The low growl grew louder.

"Show yourself, boy," Grunt said. "We won't hurt you."

He flipped the safety on his rifle to fire. The brush shook near the snare.

"C'mon, pal, what are you?"

Two reddish brown, grizzled, hood shaped ears emerged from the cover of the brush like a periscope rising on the ocean. The ears twitched and turned toward Grunt and Tucker.

Grunt spoke softly toward the animal.

"Fellow, let me see what you are."

Slowly, a flat black nose, and an angular snout appeared, followed by the head. The animal's red forelegs rose to a white chest, and a buff coat. Tucker watched the animal stare at the empty snare, and then to Grunt. They stood face to face and eye ball to eye ball.

"You…"

Tucker watched intently as Grunt seemed to freeze staring at the dog. Grunt's forehead furrowed in a question.

"Coy dog, and you think I took your supper."

Grunt lowered his rifle.

"So, we got us a Mexican standoff, pal."

The coy dog stepped cautiously on the trail.

"Big guy. You must weigh fifty or sixty pounds. Got some dog in you, all right. How much dog you got?"

The coy dog tilted his head as Grunt spoke.

"You know I'm talking about you, don't you? So, you smelled the kill, came to get it, and I beat you. Well, you know, I set the snare."

Grunt reached inside the sack, and removed the rabbit.

"Since I set the snare; it's my kill."

The coy dog howled at the sight of the rabbit. The howl echoed through the woods. The coy dog lurched a step forward. Grunt raised the rifle. The coy dog stepped back.

"So, you know guns. Judging from those scars on your front quarter, you've felt them, too."

Grunt paused. He looked down at Tucker and seemed to be searching for words to explain something. Grunt pulled back the bolt of his rifle; the brass cartridge flew out from the chamber and fell to the earth. The coy dog retreated back into the woods, with only its head in view.

"You know, all right."

Grunt picked up the cartridge, placed it in his pocket, and removed his knife from its sheath. He sliced a strip of meat from the rabbit and tossed the strip toward the animal.

"Go on, it's all right, Vo Xu. You sure as hell have her eyes; you might as well have her name."

Tucker saw furrows trace paths in the nearby brush like phosphorescent wakes across a green sea at night.

"How many are there?" Tucker asked. "And who's Vo Xu?"

Grunt spoke over his shoulder.

"Tell you later."

The coy dog looked at the meat, and then looked at Grunt. It darted to the meat, snapped it up with its sharp, white teeth clicking together, and retreated to the woods.

"Good for you. You want more?"

Grunt cut another slice of the rabbit, and tossed it to the edge of the woods.

"How hungry are you? How brave are you?"

The coy dog eyed the slice of rabbit, stepped softly on the trail, and swallowed it.

"Good, good."

The coy dog neared Grunt. Grunt cut the rabbit into more slices.

"That's our dinner," Tucker protested.

"It was. This is more important."

Grunt looked at Tucker.

"Don't worry. We won't starve tonight."

Grunt tossed the last of the rabbit to the coy dog. The coy dog gorged itself on the rabbit, and then looked back to Grunt.

"That's it, pal. You got our supper. Go skulk off and take a nap. C'mon, Tucker, least ways we got our vegetables."

Grunt and Tucker backed away from the coy dog.

The coy dog looked to the snare, and to Grunt. Grunt and the coy dog stared directly into one another's eyes.

Grunt and Tucker disappeared into the woods. The coy dog barked and leapt into the air. Grunt and Tucker walked down the trail with Grunt looking back occasionally, to see the coy dog partially hidden in the brush. "I think we got us a new friend, once she gets over her shyness."

"It's a funny looking dog."

"Part coyote, part dog, coy dog. The coyote in him makes him smart, a survivor. Damn near lives off anything. The dog in him goes all the way back to the Stone Age when men and dogs became friends. The coyote in him is telling him to be wary of us. The dog in him remembers that rabbit, and tells him there might be some good in hanging around us."

"Why did you call him Vo Xu? What kind of name is that?"

"How old you say you were?"

"Fifteen."

Grunt took a deep breath.

"Vo Xu was the name of my friend's dog in the war."

Tears formed in the corners of Grunt's eyes.

What happened to Vo Xu?"

"I'll tell you later."

"You always say that. You'll tell me later."

"I will; you'll see. I may be a lot of things, young trooper, but I'm good to my word."

Grunt nodded back toward the coy dog who was trailing them.

"Now I think that coy dog back there might be something very special."

"What do you mean?"

"Won't know for a while, but I got me a hunch about her. We sort of did the Vulcan mind meld."

Tucker laughed. He had not laughed in a very long time, and it felt very, very, good.

They continued on through the woods. Tucker looked around as he walked through the shadows of tall dark trees, and thick brush. Light filtered by the tall trees created an eerie landscape.

"This here is a very strange place, Grunt."

"I've seen some stuff in here wouldn't nobody back to town believe."

Grunt laughed.

It took Tucker and Grunt the rest of the afternoon to retrace their path out of the thick forest and to return to Grunt's cave.

Later that evening, with the sun setting, and a cool night breeze gaining strength, Grunt and Tucker sat on the cave ledge before a warming fire. Yellow and red flames licked at the stones containing them. Below the two men, at the edge of the clearing, the coy dog sat partially concealed.

Tucker pushed the cleaning rod with a small white cotton patch on it from the muzzle down the barrel through the breech of the .308 rifle. "You got it," Grunt said. "One clean motion without stopping. Get that patch all the way through. Same on the way out."

Tucker noticed that Grunt was staring at the coy dog at the edge of the clearing.

"I see you over there," Grunt said. "Do you remember me? Is that it? You guys usually don't run around alone, and I don't see your pack. That's strange."

Grunt nodded at the cleaned and oiled rifle.

"Good job, Tucker. You just may be a born woodsman."

"Thanks. I can fish, and camp, but I never learned to shoot. Can you teach me?"

"Why do you want to learn to shoot?"

"I want to get them."

"I thought you were going to say you wanted to learn how to hunt. You better think long and hard on the price before you set to killing folks."

"I don't care."

Grunt laughed.

"What's so funny?"

"If you had any idea how many folks got themselves down a big hole with no way out by saying 'I don't care.'"

Grunt waved his hand at Tucker.

"No, you don't have to explain. I know how you feel and what you meant."

"You're like a father," Tucker said.

Grunt shook as if something had struck him. He looked at Tucker. Grunt's mouth opened, but he had no words.

"I never…" Grunt's voice broke. "I never thought of me that way."

Grunt placed a large aluminum pot over the fire, and tossed in strips of venison jerky, fresh onions, and the cattail roots.

"Have us a little stew, here."

Grunt rose and went into the cave. He returned with a wineskin, two aluminum bowls, and two forks. He held the wineskin to his lips and drank down a long swig.

"Either that stuff is getting better, or I'm just getting used to it."

Grunt looked at Tucker.

"My uncle used to make dandelion wine when I was kid. Taught me how to do it. Boy, he was a woodsman. Really knew how to get by out here."

Grunt nodded at the wineskin.

"This is one thing that I am surely proud of."

"You never talk about your family?"

"We had a big fight and none of us were big enough to get over it. Never spoke to my old man after that and I heard that my mother died shortly thereafter."

Tucker nodded.

Grunt ladled out the stew into two bowls with a blue speckled finish, and handed one to Tucker.

"Eat up."

Tucker took a spoonful.

"This is good!"

Sauce trickled from the corners of his mouth.

"That's because you're hungry. You've been out in the woods all day. Glad you like it. Eat all you want."

The flicker of the flames from the fire washed across the stone ledge, draping Tucker and Grunt in its shimmering colors. Tucker looked from his bowl of stew to his buckskins, and then to Grunt. The past was very distant from Tucker at that moment.

Two eyes, crystalline red, like large glowing quartz marbles, appeared at the top of the ladder.

"Grunt," Tucker said putting down his bowl and pointing at the eyes.

"I see her," Grunt answered.

The rest of the coy dog was hidden by the night, except for the occasional wash of the firelight across her head. The coy dog whimpered with eyes wide, and ears cocked.

"I know, girl, it's more than liking my cooking. So, how close Vo Xu? How close do I let you come, girl?"

Grunt removed the pot from the fire. He took the ladle and scooped out some stew. He waved the ladle back and forth to cool the contents, and then poured the stew on a spot just before the ladder. The coy dog climbed slowly over the top of the ladder, tentatively placing its forelegs on the ledge, with its hind legs resting on the ladder to support a quick wheel and exit. She circled Grunt and Tucker, moving in and out of the firelight, appearing and disappearing as an apparition. Slowly, the coy dog circled behind Grunt, and then stopped.

The hairs on the back of Grunt's neck bristled at the touch of Vo Xu's hot, damp, breath. Her muzzle was only inches away from Grunt's weathered skin. Grunt turned and stared into her brilliant, burning eyes. She continued to circle Grunt and Tucker, and then reclined a foot away from the stew. Slowly, she inched her way forward without rising, and then eagerly, she lapped it up.

"You got more dog, than coy, girl. So, tell me, girl, how did you get to this place?"

"Grunt," Tucker said. "You don't really think that she is?"

Vo Xu sat up looking at Grunt. She belched.

"Dog after my own heart. You don't look like you got rabies. God, that'd be a hell of a way to go. Foaming at the mouth, running through the woods, insane. All right, Vo Xu, let's see if that's who you really are. C'mere, c'mere."

Grunt slapped his hand against his thigh.

The coy dog rose to her feet. She howled and looked back at the ladder.

"Come here! Come!"

Slowly, Vo Xu approached Grunt. She sniffed.

"Same smell. Same voice. Same look."

Grunt and Vo Xu stared into each other's eyes.

"It's okay; I won't hurt you. I won't. It's all right, been a long, long time, girl."

Grunt took a breath.

"A couple of lifetimes at least.

The coy dog stood in the firelight. Grunt's fingers touched her shoulders. Slowly, Grunt massaged her shoulder. His fingers ran down her chest and across her belly. Grunt felt the star shaped scars covering her chest and belly.

"Oh dear God. Oh, God."

Grunt sobbed heavily and gently pulled Vo Xu to him. She opened her jaws, and cradled his arm between them.

"It's over, girl. Nobody can ever hurt you again. Vo Xu opened her mouth, allowed Grunt to remove his arm, and then she reclined by the warm fire, laying her head on her paws staring at Grunt.

"God, Vo Xu, if you're here…can he be here, too?"

"She's that dog from the war? How can that be?" Tucker asked.

"What do you think?"

"The spirits?"

"The spirits."

Grunt rose. He turned in a circle with his arms outstretched. He nodded, and whispered his thanks to the spirits, and looked hard into the night.

CHAPTER 11
LEARNING THE SIGNS

Tucker sat on the cave ledge. Vo Xu sat patiently a few feet away with her head and forelegs touched by the warming sun, and her hindquarters draped in shadow. Heat from the rising sun lifted heavy, gray mist from the valley.

Tucker sat as far away from the cave entrance as he could without slipping off the sheer edge of the precipice to the valley below. His legs dangled over the edge. He cried softly so Grunt, still asleep inside the cave, would not hear him. Tucker awoke earlier with horrible images of the knife blades cutting across the necks of John and Amanda.

Thankful that Grunt was nowhere to be seen, Tucker allowed himself to cry. Wiping the tears from his eyes, he gazed out at a blurred and misty world of tall trees, dark shadows, and strange creatures.

Vo Xu rose, propping herself up with her forelegs, and then drawing her hind quarters beneath her, walked behind Tucker, and pushed him between the shoulders with her nose. Tucker wiped tears from his eyes, and stroked Vo Xu's ears.

"I love you, Vo Xu."

Vo Xu wagged her tail and licked Tucker's face.

"I know you love me too."

Vo Xu forced her head between Tucker's arm and his chest, wriggling next to him. Tucker's tears fell onto Vo Xu's coat. The harder Tucker embraced Vo Xu, the weaker the images of pain became.

Grunt emerged from the cave, paused to observe the scene, looking to Tucker and then Vo Xu. Grunt nodded his approval.

"Morning, young trooper."

"Morning, Grunt."

Tucker wiped the tears from his eyes.

"What are we doing today?"

"Well, we could pack us up some rations and trek on back to the world. Get you back to where you belong."

"Not today."

"We could go fishing."

Grunt grinned and looked down at Tucker.

"Teach me more about the woods?"

"I can do that."

Soon, Tucker was walking along behind Grunt down the ancient and well-traveled game path.

The morning air smelled sweet to Tucker, with the fragrance of pine and tall grass. A gentle breeze flowed across the tops of the high grass causing it to sway in the wind.

Tucker knew he wanted to be a part of this place the way that Grunt was.

Tucker glanced to his right. Something moved. At least he thought something had moved in the nearby woods.

"Grunt!"

"Yeah, Tucker."

Grunt stopped and turned around to face him.

"There is somebody following us."

"Not exactly. There's just a lot of something in those woods. Nothing for you to be afraid of."

"I'm not afraid."

"I know it; let's keep going.

Tucker looked furtively over his shoulder as they continued their passage deeper into the woods. He was sure that someone or something was following them.

By mid-morning, Grunt and Tucker sat on the riverbank of a fast moving stream, a tributary of the Gunpowder River. Faint droplets of water splashed into the air, and touched their faces in a soothing mist. The roar of the stream drowned out the background noise of the woods.

"I call her Grunt Creek."

Tucker smiled.

"Named her after myself."

"I got that. How do you know it's Grunt Creek? Maybe the Indians called it Creek of the Night Monsters."

"I don't, but seeing that it's only you and me here, I figure it's Grunt Creek."

Grunt cut two long, vibrant saplings from the earth near the trunk of an oak, trimmed the ends, and tied lines with bobbers to them.

"See if you can find us some good worms."

Tucker disappeared into the woods returning several moments later.

"I got them," Tucker said, emerging from the woods.

"Thank you."

Grunt put a fat, coiling earthworm on a hook at the end of each line.

"Here you go."

Grunt handed one of the poles to Tucker. Grunt swung his bait out into the current, which passed over a deep pool in front of them. Tucker copied Grunt's motion. The red and white plastic bobbers were tossed by the swift current into pools carved out by the river.

"Hold my fishing stick," Grunt said.

Grunt opened a small knapsack, took out a battered tin percolator, and went to the stream bed. He filled the percolator with water, returned, and started a small fire ringed by rocks. Soon the fire was burning, and the brown liquid was percolating. After a while, Grunt reached down to the battered tin percolator and poured Beechnut coffee into two metal cups, and handed one to Tucker.

Tucker handed one of the fishing sticks to Grunt, and Grunt handed him a cup.

"Thank you, Grunt," Tucker said.

Tucker's bobber went under.

"Whoa, young trooper, you got one."

The sapling bent in half with Tucker pulling hard on one end, and the trout pulling hard on the other end to escape. Tucker set the hook and pulled a fat Rainbow Trout out of the stream.

"Good job, young trooper."

Grunt filleted the trout, cut open its stomach out of curiosity to see what it was feeding on, and then laid the two fillets across a green sapling in the shape of a "Y". The fish cooked quickly. The two ate with their fingers, flakes of flesh falling to the earth, and then Grunt extinguished the fire, and poured out the coffee pot. He lowered the pot into the rushing water to cool it, and then put it in his pack.

"Let's head back. We'll get back…"

"Home," Tucker said.

Grunt smiled and nodded.

Tucker kept pace with Grunt, lagging only a yard behind him. At a turn in the trail, Tucker noticed a pile of rustling orange and yellow leaves.

Tucker watched raptly as a creature's reddish skin appeared in the dim, refracted sunlight. A narrow moving field of dull red took on an angular shape; a round edged arrowhead, several inches thick, coursed across the earth. He looked into the twin, tiny black eyes framed within the contours of the red head. Staring up at Tucker, the eyes peered weakly across the distance. Tentatively, the serpent's brown, hour glass pattern emerged from the cover of dark shadow and rotting leaves to ripple slowly across the trail. The creature's movements were slow, well defined, and defiant. The muscles in Tucker's right ankle and foot constricted.

The Copperhead slowly lifted its head, tasted the air with its slender, black tongue, and paused. The twin black pits of its eyes looked up at Tucker the instant its body touched the boy's boot. Tucker stared at the tiny eyes of this creature that appeared as if it were contemplating whether to speak to him or not.

Tucker strained his ears, listening carefully, just in case there were words to come to him. After pausing, the rippling life of the snake coursed across Tucker's still flesh. Somehow, Tucker felt there was a bond between the two of them. Despite the lethal liquid it carried in the sacs behind its fangs, this Copperhead had willingly exposed the entire length of its sinuous, coursing self to this creature blocking its path. He thought of raising a stone or stick and striking it down quick, hard, and fatally against the snake's head, and then the thought just as quickly vanished in the wake of the wave of fascination. A faint tremor signaled the passage of the three foot long snake across his foot as it passed from darkness into light and then back into darkness. He stood transfixed by the sight and the touch of the serpent.

Chills coursed down the channel of his spine, lingering, and then fading as the snake slithered away. Tucker looked up to see Grunt waiting for him at the top of the trail. Hurriedly, Tucker ran up the trail.

"You did well," Grunt said, looking back down the trail.

"Most things out here are more than happy to leave you alone if you're smart enough to leave them alone. What do you think he'd have done if you'd gone after him with a stick?"

"Bite me?"

"Yeah, more than likely."

Tucker watched Grunt eye him up and down.

"Somebody your size, make you awful sick, might even kill you."

Grunt turned and slowly led Tucker back toward the cave. They moved without words through a one hundred foot tall stand of Eastern White Pine.

Above them, the horizontal branches of the pine trees, dotted with yellowish brown cones rustled pleasingly in the wind. To Tucker, the sound was that of tranquil sea, and a he a privateer in league with a brave captain.

Grunt waved at Tucker, and then sat down with his back leaning against a tree. Tucker sat near him.

"Why did you pick this valley?" Tucker asked.

The wind grew in intensity, tossing Tucker's hair, and plucking the words from his mouth before they were completely formed.

"I think she picked me."

Grunt looked up at the dark canopy, and around the trunks of the tall pines at the thicker forest beyond. Shadow and sunlight fell through the deep woods, casting everything in black and white.

"Things in life are like that, young trooper."

Grunt took his water skin from his shoulder, and handed it to Tucker. Tucker accepted it, removed the stopper, and held it a few inches from his open mouth. He drank.

"It was meant for my family to be killed?" Tucker asked.

"I don't believe in accidents and coincidences. Oh, I think you can work around the edges a bit, but there's a plan."

"It was meant for my family to be killed?" Tucker repeated.

"We all die, Tucker."

"Dying isn't killing."

"No, it certainly isn't."

Grunt patted Tucker on the shoulder.

"That's a pretty good distinction you just made there."

Brush at the side of the game trail shook with a flash of green, and cracked with the brittle, rattle of branch on branch. Looking down in the damp, fresh brown mud of the trail, Truth saw the still fresh imprints, slender tracks nearly three inches long like angled tear drops covering the trail.

"Herd came through here in a hurry," Grunt said.

He knelt.

"Something was after them to run like this. Old bucks mixed in with females and young ones. They were moving pell-mell away from something."

"What?"

"Maybe wolves."

Grunt rose, and moved to the edge of the trail, parting the brush with his right arm. A young White-tailed Deer, its head, neck, back, and sides a dull red-brown, and the rest of it white, was prostrate. One of its forelegs was obviously broken. Grunt motioned for Tucker to come forward. The deer was in great pain from the broken leg with impending death certain. The animal eyed Grunt and Tucker with mute resignation.

"What do we need to do?" Grunt asked.

"We can't leave him like this. It wouldn't be right. He won't live, will he?"

"No. Suffer mightily until something comes along and dispatches him. Don't get too close. All the pain he's in, he can still come at you with those hooves. Remember what I showed you when you cleaned it?"

"Yes."

Grunt handed his rifle to Tucker, its weight pulling down the boy's arms. Grunt helped Tucker wedge the butt of the rifle into his shoulder, and place the stock next to his cheek. Tucker's face grew solemn, and questioning; looking at the deer, at the rifle cradled within his arms, and then at Grunt.

"One shot, back of the head. Clean and quick; brace yourself against that tree."

Grunt pulled back the bolt; pushed it forward, chambering a bright, brass round accompanied by a metal click.

Tucker stepped back, leaned against the rough bark of a wide, old pine, fitted the rifle butt into his shoulder, raised the rifle, hesitated, aimed and fired. The rifle butt jolted back into Tucker's right shoulder sending a jagged shard of hot pain into his flesh. The explosion pained his ears. The report of the rifle echoed through the forest as the gray wisps of gun smoke hung in the air. Grunt placed his hand on Tucker's shoulder.

"Good. Now, I'll show you how to gut and clean him. We don't leave anything for waste out here. Besides that, if we just left him, it wouldn't honor him. Food from him will be part of us."

"That sounds like something an Indian would say."

Grunt smiled. He hung the deer from a tree limb by a rope noose around its hind legs.

"Watch me close. As long as you're out here, you need to know these things."

Grunt made a long incision, slitting the deer's throat. Fresh warm blood dripped to the cold earth, and a mist rose from its passage. Tucker inhaled the sweet, sticky scent of the deer's blood. Grunt made a ring cut at the joints of the legs; cutting the skin from the belly to the throat wound. Tucker saw his image reflected on the blade as Grunt cut down the forelegs and traced a circle around the young male's sex organs. Replacing the knife in its sheath, Grunt grasped the hide of the deer and pulled it from the carcass. Removing his knife from the leather sheaf, he cut into the belly, removing the entrails.

"Come here."

Tucker stood by Grunt.

"That is the liver; don't puncture it. We do that, the meat is ruined. Now, roll up your sleeves, reach inside there, and pull out the insides."

"Okay."

Tucker took a deep breath, held it, and then reached inside and removed the organs. The still warm entrails of the deer seemed to wrap themselves over and around Tucker's arms. Slowly, as if he were cradling a bomb in his arms, Tucker walked a short way down the trail, and then angled his arms down to allow the warm, damp organs to slide from him. They slapped against the earth, sending back drops of the dead animal's essence to fall upon Tucker's cheeks.

"Little stream over there; go wash yourself off."

Grunt sat back down against a tree and watched as Tucker washed up. Tucker returned from the stream.

"Good job, young trooper. You'll make it out here."

Grunt placed the venison inside the hide, and tied it tightly.

"Why are you looking at me funny?"

"Nothing, Tucker. Manners are sort of rusty."

Grunt chuckled.

"Don't need many manners when you're entertaining bears and wolves."

"How do you entertain bears and wolves?" Tucker asked.

"By running like a human. They laugh their asses off when they see how slow and clumsy we are. Sometimes, that's why they let us get away. They feel sorry for us. All right, let's get moving."

Tucker followed Grunt down along the banks of the Gunpowder River. The footing was treacherous as they walked over mist-draped boulders and moss-covered stones.

"There."

Grunt knelt in the damp sand by the water.

"C'mon down here, Tucker. Lesson two, tracking." Over his shoulder he nodded at Tucker to join him.

"What do you see? C'mon, get down; look closer."

Tucker descended the bank.

"Looks like somebody's been eating crayfish. Shells on the sand."

"Good. Now, what else do you see?"

"Prints. I don't know them."

"Okay, what animals do you think would hunt for crayfish?"

"Bears?" Tucker said looking warily around him at the dark woods.

"Yeah, they could. Some guys with stripes and a bandit face could too."

"Raccoons?"

"Yeah. Look, see five toes on the front and rear paws. Front paw is smaller, more like a hand. Take a good look. That's a raccoon."

Grunt bent down low and sniffed the earth.

"Not long ago; scent is still fresh. Let's keep going. Okay, that's a print. Now, look for scat."

"Scat?"

"Poop. Tell a lot about an animal by looking at their poop."

"Is this a joke?"

"No, scat and we'll know what did it."

Tucker took a couple of steps.

"Here, looks like dog poop."

"Good. Course there aren't too many dogs running loose out here. See those prints?"

"Two toes, no four toes, and its foot."

"Four toes and the pad. So?"

"Not a dog?"

"Not a dog."

"Coyote or a wolf?"

"Okay, which?"

"Is a wolf's print bigger?"

"Yes."

"Coyote."

Grunt slapped Tucker on the shoulder.

"Good. C'mon; let's get back while we got sunlight."

Grunt hefted the venison onto his shoulder.

"I want to get started smoking this meat before dark."

After several hours of fast walking Grunt and Tucker emerged into the clearing by the cave. The poultice that Grunt had applied to Tucker's feet had worked extremely well, and the cuts on Tucker's feet were almost healed.

"C'mon over here."

Tucker stopped next to Grunt by a hole in the ground that was roughly three feet across and three feet deep.

"We need to stack up some dry firewood here."

Grunt pointed to one side of the hole.

"Then, on the other side, stack up some green wood."

"Green wood doesn't burn well?" Tucker asked.

"You're right."

Grunt smiled at Tucker and Tucker returned the smile.

"We get the fire going with the dry stuff, drop in the green wood to make her smoke, and then put our grate…"

Grunt lifted a wooden rectangle of straight branches tied together with deer hide.

"…over the top. Smoke from the green wood will start to cure the meat."

Grunt knelt, unrolled the hide covering the venison, and then took a hunting knife from his belt. He handed the knife to Tucker.

"Here, start cutting thin, narrow slices about as wide as your pinky."

Tucker knelt. He slowly cut thin strips. Grunt went off into the nearby woods and returned with dry firewood. He made repeated trips until a large stack was by the fire pit.

"Okay."

Grunt wiped sweat from his forehead. Suddenly, he shook his right hand and winced.

"You all right?"

"Hurt myself. Good job, keep cutting those strips. I'll go get some green wood."

Grunt built a large pile of green wood next to the fire pit, and then sat down. He leaned down and placed kindling at the bottom of the pit, lit it with a disposable lighter, and then fed it with larger branches. He turned, laid the grate before him, and then neatly laid the thin strips of venison that Tucker had cut across the grate.

"Good job. Now put some of that green wood on the fire. Here's the trick, we want it to smoke, but we don't want to put so much green stuff down there that it puts out the fire."

"Okay."

Tucker took green twigs from the pile that Grunt had built, and then laid them down on the fire. Smoke rose.

Grunt placed the grate over the fire.

"Guess what we're doing for tonight and tomorrow night?"

"Smoking deer meat?"

"Yeah,"

said Grunt laying back and looking up at the evening sky. A nearly full moon appeared in the twilight.

"Should keep the meat for a couple of weeks."

"I wondered what we were going to do with the meat out here. Too much for one night."

"Well, we'll put a couple of venison steaks on the fire tonight."

As if on cue Vo Xu's head appeared at the edge of the clearing.

"Yeah, girl," Grunt said. "You'll get a steak, too."

Later that evening, after they had eaten, Tucker and Grunt sat on the ledge before the cave with a small fire burning.

"How did you learn all of this?" Tucker asked.

"I knew some when I was kid. Grew up on a farm. Used to go rabbit hunting with shotgun when I was eight years old. Like I told you before, it was really my uncle who taught me. Learned some in the army. Mostly about survival."

Grunt waved his arm at the valley.

"Then, when I got out here I learned a lot by trial and error. What didn't kill you made you smarter."

A far off owl called.

Tucker, his arm around Vo Xu, watched Grunt smile.

"Listen," said Grunt.

The grin on his face grew broader. He took in a deep breath, cupped his hands to his mouth, and sang back to the owl with a string of cylindrical notes chained together in a regular pulse of crescendos.

Tucker listened as the notes rose from Grunt, spun through the firelight, and then disappeared in the night. "Hoot, hoot, hoot-hoot, hoot."

Grunt pointed to the black wall of trees.

"Listen."

To Tucker's amazement, at the other end of the arc of sound, the owl answered back.

"Hoot, hoot, hoot-hoot, hoot."

Tucker laughed and Grunt smiled.

"Hoot, hoot, hoot-hoot, hoot."

Grunt waved his finger in front of his chest as if he were calling for time from Tucker.

"Okay, okay, that's his call. That's the call of the Great Horned Owl. He's about yea high."

Grunt motioned with his right hand above his left hand as if he were carrying a vase two feet tall. He rubbed his shoulders and chest.

"He's all dark brown and gray," and then stroked his throat, "and he's got this beautiful white throat." He took a deep breath. "Hoot, hoot....", and then craned his neck to listen.

"Hoot-hoot, hoot."

"There he goes, Tucker. He's talking to us."

Grunt continued.

"He's got big old ear tufts sticking out, the better for him to hear, and a pair of yellow eyes. I tell you, you be a rabbit or a grouse and you see those yellow eyes coming out of the night, that's the last thing you'll see."

The call of the Great Horned Owl continued as Tucker stared into the night sky. Whatever Grunt had said to him, or asked, the owl had plenty to say in response.

"Why did you end up here?"

"I guess I was a war leper. We came home alone, one at time. We'd already become someone else. We were just renting the bodies we were in. But, we didn't know that. We'd find out when we got back. You could see it in the eyes of the people who thought they knew us. We didn't talk the same, drink the same, make...do a lot of things the same. They didn't know us. Worse than being back was leaving the others behind, deserting them when it came our time."

"If you didn't come home, you could have died there."

"Worse things than dying."

"I don't get it. What could be worse?"

Tucker rose, stepped closer to Grunt, and gently placed his hand on the older man's shoulder.

"If you're dead, you can't do anything. All these years, you still feel bad?"

"Yeah, Tucker. My life ended when I was twenty two."

Melancholia over the death of his parents and grandparents sought its cold hold on Tucker's soul. Grunt had paid a terrible price. Tucker could see that. Tucker had paid his own terrible price in losing his parents and grandparents.

Tucker felt close to this very different man. Tucker had never known anyone like this. Tucker would find some kind of peace within this valley, as Grunt did. For now, he was safe. Each day his thoughts were focused on the present and not the past.

"Okay," Grunt said. "Why don't you go on down and check on the fire? Then we can go to bed. I'll go down a couple of times tonight to make sure the fire says lit and smoky."

"How you going to do that? We don't have a clock."

"Yeah we do," Grunt said pointing up at the constellation of Cassiopeia. Grunt pointed with his right hand, and again Tucker noticed him wince.

"Can you find the North Star?"

"It's north."

"Yeah, can you point it out?"

"Not sure."

"C'mon over here."

Tucker got up, walked over, and sat down next to Grunt.

"Find the Big Dipper."

"I got it," Tucker said.

"How many stars?"

"Seven."

"You got it. Now, look down to the bucket, and line up the two stars at the back of the bucket."

"Okay."

"Now, just look up on a line from those two stars until you see it."

"North Star," Tucker said.

"Good. Now, look on off to the right. Look for what seems like a 'W.' Go on a line from the North Star to a bright star in the middle of a group of five."

"Got it," Tucker said.

"That my young friend is Cassiopeia. That's my clock."

"How?"

"All night long it will circle around the North Star. You watch it move, and you'll figure out the time. Right now it's about nine o'clock."

"That's neat," Tucker said. "How's your hand?"

"Oh, it'll be all right. You go see to the fire at our smoke pit, and then I'll check on it the rest of the night."

CHAPTER 12

THE HARVEST

Jim paced on the porch of the ramshackle cabin. Sweat matted his long hair against his neck. His clothes were filthy from harvesting the last of the marijuana plants. Through the stained polypropylene sheet tacked to the window frame he watched Mike and Dan scooping marijuana leaves into small plastic bags, place them on scales, adjust the weight of the contents, and then seal the bags. On the floor next to the crude table were cardboard boxes. The boxes were nearly full of neatly packed and stacked bags.

"Almost as good as robots," Jim said to himself. "Not as smart, but almost as good."

Jim pulled upon the door, and stepped into the cabin.

"All right, you guys done good. Let's load that stuff up on the ATV's. Mike, you and me are going to take that to the stash at the edge of the woods. Dan, you're the best tracker of all of us. I want you to find out where Grunt and the boy are. After me and Mike get back we'll settle up with those too."

"Are we going to kill them both?" Dan asked.

"Again?" Jim said. "We might have a chance if it was just Grunt saw us. He ain't about to go running into town and talking. But that kid? We got to bank on him surfacing in town, and if he does, that'll force the law to come in here. Get it?"

"Yeah. How long before you're back?" Dan said.

"Most of what's left of today to get out. Stash it. Then back. Figure two days. Pack up what you need, and in two days we'll meet you back here. Think you can find Grunt and the boy?"

"I'll find them, but I sure don't like being in those woods alone."

"Here," Jim said angrily taking the key to the ATV. "You take the dope out and I'll go find him."

"No, I'm sorry, boss. I'll do it."

Dan checked his rifle, tossed some canned goods and extra ammunition into his pack, and then stuffed in his sleeping bag. He opened the door, paused, and turned to look at the others.

"Two days?"

"Two days."

Jim and Mike got on the ATVs. The engines started with a disconcerting roar against the quiet of the woods.

Dan stood watching his cohorts disappear down a game trail. It was early afternoon, and Dan figured he'd get back to where they had killed John and Amanda Pierce, track the boy up to the hill where Grunt had intervened, and then track from there to wherever Grunt lived.

Dan exhaled a deep breath at the thought of confronting Grunt.

Not alone, for damn sure I'm not going after him alone. Like going into a bear's cave alone. No, I'll find them, won't let them see me, and then I'll get on back and get Jim and Mike.

Dan trekked along for hours. Passing through the Gunpowder Creek he filled his gallon size water bag. As the light in the forest grew dimmer, Dan's thoughts went to a secure place for the night.

No fire. He was too close to wherever Grunt was. Several hours before he'd crested the ridge where he had last seen Grunt and the boy. He'd found where they had rummaged for plants and where they'd gone fishing. At dusk, like a predator seeking prey, Dan raised his head and caught the scent of smoking venison. Dan continued on until it became too dark for him to go any further that night.

He climbed atop a large boulder, smoothed away the surface, and spread out his sleeping bag. Nearby he saw through the woods to a clearing and what looked like a pit with smoke coming out of it.

He had a three hundred and sixty degree view of his surroundings. Quickly opening a can of vegetable beef soup, he ate the soup without heating it or adding water, and threw the empty can as far from his camp as he could. He listened to it crash into the distant brush, and then he went to sleep.

They got to be close. Real close.

He failed to notice a pair of red eyes fixed on him from the nearby woods.

CHAPTER 13

ALMOST DOWN

Tucker stared at Grunt walking slowly back to the fire pit on the rock ledge. The hissing fire cast tiger striped shadows across Grunt. Grunt's eyes seemed narrower, and the skin across his face was drawn tight. He held his left wrist with his right hand. Tucker saw clearly that Grunt was afraid. Grunt's fear kindled corresponding fears in Tucker. Tucker was afraid for his friend, and was afraid for himself. Tucker was afraid that he would do the wrong thing and cause Grunt's death. If something went wrong this night Tucker feared for his survival. Then, Tucker realized how selfish that was. Grunt was in need, and Tucker was the only one who could help him. Tucker inhaled deeply.

"I want to thank you, Grunt…"

"Whoa, young trooper. Let's not tempt the fates here."

Grunt looked to the night sky.

"Let's not start any goodbyes just yet."

"Okay."

Tucker was embarrassed.

"I guess we ought to get ready to do this. It sure ain't going to get any better on its own."

Tucker watched Grunt grimace extending his left hand showing the stained white cloth wrapped around his swollen index finger.

"Do we need to go through it again?"

"Yes please."

Tucker didn't need to rehearse the surgery again, but he did want to postpone doing it as long as he could.

"Okay," said Grunt said. "First, you got to sterilize both these hunting knives."

Grunt pointed to two hunting knives with seven inch blades and worn deer antler hafts.

"Place the blades in the fire until we're sure we get them sterilized."

Grunt smiled.

"The last damn thing we want to do is get this thing cut clean off and then have an infection set in."

Grunt spit off into the night.

"Then, you take the first one, place the blade just above and behind the knuckle, and gently just touch the edge of the blade to the skin. With your other hand, take that hatchet, and bring her down fast and hard against the knife. One blow through this knuckle."

Grunt took a deep breath.

"Tucker, man, I love you like a son, but I may say all sorts of things while this is happening. Ignore them. This is the quick part right here. Once you cut that part of my finger cut off, you got to get that other blade quick and place the flat of the red hot blade against the bloody stump. Lots of blood will be spilling out fast. Don't pay it no never mind. You got to be quick and focused and press that blade against the flesh to seal it. Got it?"

"I got it Grunt."

"I'm sure you do. I'll put my hand on this chopping block over here by the fire. You'll take the first knife, and chop, and then the second and seal the wound. Why don't you set yourself down and get comfortable. Practice a little bit reaching for the first knife, doing the chop, and then reaching for the second."

Tucker sat between the fire and Grunt. He reached toward the fire where he would put the two knives. Then, he used his right hand to simulate picking up the first knife and holding it over Grunt's finger.

"Good, good. Damn blood poisoning. Just won't keep any longer and we don't have time to get to town. I was hoping it would cure itself up, but I guess I knew it wouldn't."

Grunt lifted the first of two long bladed hunting knives by his side, and carefully slipped the blade into the coals. Then, he took the second knife and inserted its blade into the coals as well.

Grunt unwrapped the bandage slowly. He mumbled to himself in pain as he unrolled the stained cloth.

"Got to come off up to that knuckle, my friend."

Grunt looked down at a small box of gauge bandages, a small bottle of hydrogen peroxide, and a tube of ointment. The last item was a fifth of bourbon whiskey.

"Been saving this for a special occasion, but this isn't quite what I had in mind."

Grunt moved the chopping block from shadow into the firelight. He placed a leather strap next to it, and then took long swallows from the bottle.

"Be patient, my friend," Grunt said pausing between swallows. "I'm sure glad you're here."

Tucker stared up at the cold, white stars tightly packed against the black, night sky. The Milky Way was a shimmering highway to somewhere or something. Cassiopeia made its revolving course through the night sky. He figured he had been waiting an hour for Grunt to drink down as much of the bourbon as he needed as a pain killer. He mentally rehearsed what he would do when Grunt was ready.

"Okay, young trooper. I'm ready."

Grunt laid his left hand on the stump.

"I don't want you to die," Tucker said.

"Me neither. Just do what you got to do."

Grunt managed a weak smile.

"I got faith in you, son."

Grunt took a leather strap and running it underneath the chopping block and across his arm, tied his wrist down tight, and pulled the leather strap tight with his right hand and teeth.

"You ready, Grunt?"

"Do it, before I decide to just go in a fever and delirium."

Grunt tossed the stained dressing into the fire. The fire hissed. Tucker removed the first knife from the fire allowing the second to remain and to glow red hot. Tucker held the razor sharp blade glowing red a few inches above Grunt's swollen and festering finger in his right hand. With his left hand he took the hatchet, and held it with the flat head just above the knife.

"Do her, son." Grunt looked away.

Tucker swallowed hard. His throat was dry as he brought the blade down just touching Grunt's skin. When he was confident the edge of the blade was where he wanted it, Tucker struck hard and fast severing Grunt's third finger between the second and third joint. The partial digit rolled off the wooden stump and fell on the ledge. The metal blade made a hard thudding sound striking the wood and causing Tucker to feel queasy in the pit of his stomach. He felt as if a cold stone was in his stomach, and saliva filled his mouth.

Grunt struggled reflexively but kept his bloody stump still. Bright red blood full of oxygen soaked Grunt's hand and the top of the stump. Tears filled Tucker's eyes, and his body shook with fear, but he resolved not to cry out embarrassing himself before Grunt.

"Quickly, son," Grunt said through clenched teeth. "Quickly now."

Tucker took the second knife from the fire, grasped the hilt with both hands, and quickly and firmly pressed its red, glowing flat edge, against Grunt's bleeding wound. The cauterized flesh hissed and burned as the fire purified the wound and sealed it. Grunt screamed in pain, collapsed, and removed the restraining leather.

"You done good, son," Grunt said breathlessly.

Tucker placed the second knife next to the first one on a stone by the fire. His hands shook as he sat against the fire pit.

Grunt writhed on the ground attempting to curl into a fetal position screaming in agony. The scream echoed from the clearing up the river and into the woods. Tucker moved over and knelt next to Grunt placing his hands on his shoulders.

"Okay, wrap her up now." Grunt panted.

Grunt laid his wrist on the chopping block with his left hand extending off into space.

Tucker wrapped the clean gauze around the wound, and then quickly taped it. Grunt nodded and then crawled away from the fire on his knees and right hand. He vomited spewing partly digested venison, and bourbon onto the rocks. Vo Xu ran to him and licked his neck.

Tucker watched Grunt roll onto his back and stare through tearing eyes at the brilliant stars against the night sky.

"Oh god, man, give me the bottle."

Tucker took the bourbon bottle and brought it to Grunt. Hungrily, Grunt brought the bottle to his lips and drank down the fiery brown liquid.

Suddenly, Tucker lost control. Rushing to the side of the cliff, Tucker fell to his knees and vomited. Tucker's vision was hazy with tears. His throat was dry and constricted.

Within the fog of his vision, Tucker saw the indistinct form of a soldier wearing jungle fatigues standing before him, in mid-air. The soldier appeared to be in his late teens or early twenties. He wore a jungle hat with a cut down brim. One word was written in heavy block letters on his hat. TRUTH. He had a necklace of white beads around his neck, a Montagnard brass bracelet on his wrist, and a deep tan. He was smiling.

"Don't take him, yet."

Tucker prayed wondering if this apparition were an angel. The shape seemed to understand what Tucker had said.

Tucker went inside the cave and then returned with two wool blankets. He placed one on Grunt, and then lay down by the side of the fire. Vo Xu settled herself on the blanket next to Tucker. Tucker rested his arm on Vo Xu's back.

Tucker leaned back staring at Grunt. He resolved to stay awake all night in case Grunt needed his help. Tucker's gaze traveled up to the Milky Way, and then fell back to earth. As he closed his eyes, just for a moment, he saw the image of the young soldier who seemed to be hovering by Grunt.

Within seconds, despite his good intentions, Tucker was fast asleep.

CHAPTER 14

A MORAL WEIGHT

Tucker awoke at the sound of Grunt gnashing his teeth and moaning. The moans were deep and ghoulish like the sounds of a mortally wounded animal crying out for others of its kind.

Tucker was startled. Was Grunt about to die? Had they failed in trying to heal him? Tucker had vowed to himself to keep his eye on Grunt through the night, but he had failed him.

Tucker looked up at Cassiopeia. Its five bright stars had wheeled halfway around the night sky. Tucker estimated that it was now four o'clock in the morning. A hint of dawn was in the eastern sky. Propping himself up on his left elbow Tucker looked through the rippling heat waves rising from the low fire. Tucker was unsure of what to do.

Grunt rocked back and forth with the blanket clutched tightly around him. He didn't seem to be awake. The disturbances of the others caused Vo Xu to sit up at the edge of the dim circle of light.

Someone or something sat next to Grunt. Tucker was transfixed by what he saw. Fear and fascination caused him to rub his fists against his closed eyes, and then look again. It was the soldier that Tucker had seen before. The outline was faint, and Tucker stared through the shape to the dark woods beyond. As he stared at the figure, it took on more density until it was finally opaque. The soldier wore a faded jungle hat. Tucker read the word TRUTH hand printed in block letters across the front. Pale red rust stains from spare grenade rings attached to the exterior band spotted the hat. The man's long sandy blonde hair fell out over his ears. His skin was tanned like leather. He was slender. He seemed to Tucker to be like a coiled spring ready to explode.

"Oh, man, Truth. Truth. Truth. Man, I didn't mean to. I didn't. Man."

Tears flooded Grunt's face. His back shook as he sobbed. Wiping the tears from his eyes he stared into the face of the apparition before him. His gaze passed through the form of the soldier. Grunt's hair was matted with sweat. Tears wet his face. His rocking back and forth grew more intense. He cradled his left hand in the palm of his right hand.

Grunt appeared to Tucker to be in a trance. He seemed totally focused on the spirit before him and oblivious to the presence of Tucker and Vo Xu.

"Truth, man, I'm sorry man. I wish it were me."

Grunt cried hard.

"All these years I wished it was me."

Tucker knelt near Grunt unsure of what to do. Was Grunt having a nightmare? Was he awake? Tentatively, Tucker reached out and placed his hand on Grunt's shoulder.

"Truth, man? Is that you? Are you here? Are you really here? You can't be here. Maybe I'm drunk. Maybe I'm seeing things."

Grunt shook his head vigorously as if to clear his vision.

"I'm here," Truth said, "It's me."

Grunt sank back under the weight of a voice he had not heard since the day when everything went very wrong.

"God, Truth, we didn't have to go down that road. I couldn't understand what Six said on the radio. I figured it was a milk run anyway. We were just going down the road, blow up a few mines, and come back and drink a few beers. We were out with the Cav that day.

Riding on ACAVs. Then I heard that explosion. I turned and looked back. Our guys leaped out of the vehicles rolling onto the ground and firing into the rocks. Rounds going everywhere. Fifties opened up. M16's firing. All around me, men on their bellies firing into the jungle. Brass cartridge casings flying from the weapons, firing bursts. Gray smoke rising around us. Down the road behind us thick, black smoke broiling out of the split belly of the ACAV. Crater in the road filled with oil. I didn't want to look but I couldn't turn away. Yellow flames licking the skin of that upside down beast. I could see, it was upside down! I was looking for you! I couldn't see you; I didn't know where you were. Screams. Guys running down the road toward the ACAV, dropping empty magazines to the ground, jamming in loaded ones, and firing again. Gunners on the ACAVs crouched behind thin metal plates, firing until the barrels of the machine guns glowed red. Then, it was over. Then, I found you."

Truth nodded. He crossed his arms over his chest.

"You were dying and didn't know it. Looking up like a baby in a crib looking around. You had this funny look on your face. It was like you were smiling on the way out. You seemed too peaceful. All the noise and smoke and smell of diesel around me. And you were like an island of slow motion silence in the middle of it all. Your mouth trembled. I knew you were trying to find words, but couldn't. Your lips were moving around but nothing came out. The ACAV burned behind us covering us in smoke, small arms rounds were popping off and flying over our heads. Why? Why wasn't it me? I was on the first vehicle past the mine, it should have been me. And then you died. You were gone. I crouched there with your blood soaking me until others pulled me off. I watched them zip you up in a body bag. Carry you to a Huey landing down the road. Your death was on me, Truth."

"I know."

"Do you know? All these years, do you know? I'm sorry! Sorry! Sorry!"

"It didn't have to be," Grunt said.

"War didn't have to be," Truth said.

"Man, I'm sorry, sorry, sorry. If I could do it again…"

"It's over. I forgive you."

Truth smiled.

"It don't mean nothing."

Truth's image faded from sight.

Tucker pressed hard on Grunt's shoulders. Grunt rolled to his side, and then sat up. He was still deep in his delirium. Grunt embraced Tucker placing his head on his shoulder.

Grunt cried softly. His shoulders heaved.

"What?"

Grunt suddenly awoke.

"What are we?"

Grunt pushed Tucker away, and then looked around the rock ledge.

"You had a nightmare."

Tucker moved back from Grunt, and eyed the spot where the spirit had been.

"Oh, man, I haven't had one like that in years."

Grunt paused. He looked back to where Truth had been."Did you see him?"

"Yes, I did. Who is Truth?"

"Oh, God. It was real. Somehow it was all real." Grunt fell back against the rock ledge clutching the blanket. What little strength he had left drained away.

Tucker watched Grunt fall fast asleep. With a glance up to Cassiopeia, Tucker returned to his blanket, and he too fell asleep.

After what seemed only a few minutes, Tucker became aware of light crawling over the hills in the east. Rubbing his eyes, he saw Grunt, with Vo Xu sitting faithfully by him. Grunt was shaking his head and rubbing his face with his right hand. Tucker went to Grunt, and knelt next to him and Vo Xu. Grunt looked down at his wrist. The black lines from blood poisoning were gone.

"I'm gonna' be just fine, young trooper. Body and soul."

"Who was Truth?"

"James P. Monroe. Truth."

Grunt gestured as if he were writing a word on hat.

"We served together. One day we were ordered to go down a road. We were on armored cavalry vehicles. A few kilometers down the road the third vehicle, the one that Truth was riding on, went over a five hundred pound bomb. All the crew and Truth were killed. He died in my arms on the side of the road."

"That was a long time ago."

"A very long time, and only yesterday."

Tucker turned around three hundred and sixty degrees.

"First Vo Xu, and then Truth. This is one strange place."

He continued to turn.

"You got stuff popping out from the shadows."

CHAPTER 15

AIM

The morning mist had lifted through the tops of the tall pines by the time Tucker and Grunt made their way to Grunt's makeshift firing range.

"The most important thing is breathing," Grunt said.

He knelt on the dry earth. With his right hand he drew a roller coaster path of three curves with a stick.

"Nobody can hold the sights on the target without moving. You breathe in and out, your chest rises and falls. So, here's what you do. Inhale, exhale, inhale, exhale, hold your breath for a second when the front sight is on the target, and press the trigger. Got it."

"I got it."

"Okay. That .308 is a might big for you, so prop yourself up against a tree. Don't think about the recoil. Get a good sight picture, watch your breathing, and then press the trigger. The gun going off ought to be a surprise to you."

Tucker rested the rifle on the limb of a small pine. Fifty yards away Grunt had leaned a rotten log against a tree trunk, and driven a short, squat stick into the rotten log to serve as a target.

"Got the target?"

Tucker looked through the rear sight blade and across the front sight blade.

"I see it," Tucker said coldly.

There before him on the wooden target Tucker saw one of the faces of the three killers. Slowly, Tucker breathed in and then breathed out watching the front sight blade until it was centered in the rear sight notch. He pressed the trigger. The recoil slammed the rifle butt into his shoulder. The report of the rifle echoed across the forest. Tucker grinned.

"You saw him, didn't you?"

"I hate them," Tucker said through clenched teeth.

Tucker's arms shook and his breath came heavy with rage.

"Hate will eat you up."

Grunt walked to Tucker. He stood looming over the boy.

"I'm going to get them."

"No doubt."

Grunt shook his head.

"What? What is it? You don't think I'm right?"

"Right has nothing to do with it. You get killing in your heart it'll turn it stone. You get filled with hate it'll blind you to love."

"You killed people."

"I was a soldier. I didn't hate them. Hell, I respected them a lot of the time for how they fought. What you're embarking on is a whole different thing."

Grunt took a deep breath.

"It's probably all academic anyway."

"Academic?"

"I mean we aren't going to get an answer for it now. I've lived up to my end. Taught you how to get by some out here."

Grunt nodded toward the target.

"Taught you how to shoot. Now, it's time I get you back."

Grunt looked down at his finger.

"And you, my friend, your sure lived up to your end of the bargain. I don't think I would have made it without you."

Grunt extended his right hand to Tucker, and they shook hands.

"Let's head back."

"Okay."

Tucker walked alongside Grunt.

"You know, I'm going to have to smoke some more venison and fish and lay up a large stock of firewood. Going to have to take a couple of trips into town to stock up on the necessities to get through winter. Probably make a couple of trips getting freeze dried food to help get me through the winter. Once the snow comes, comes for sure and stays long about December, it'll be tough getting around out here. Snowshoes and all."

Tucker listened to Grunt take a deep breath."Probably go in the morning."

"I know. I got to go back."

"I have surely enjoyed your company. But, we have a pact."

"A pact. I know."

"Why don't you come with me?" Tucker asked.

"I will."

"No, I mean stay."

"Stay?"

Grunt shook his head.

"This is all I know."

"There was a time when you didn't."

"That was a long, long time ago."

"I don't think Truth wants you to stay out here anymore."

"Truth?"

"The other night when we fixed your finger. Afterwards you had a nightmare."

Tucker watched the expression on Grunt's face become one of pain and sorrow.

"You were talking to Truth."

"So, you do know."

"I do."

Tucker looked up at the night sky.

"It's funny," Grunt said. "I felt different when I woke up that morning. I feel different now. Can it be over, after all these years? And if it is, then what?"

Unbeknownst to Tucker, Dan looked up at the wood door to Grunt's cave, the fire pit on the ledge, and the smoke pit at the base of the clearing.

"Son a bitch," he said softly to himself. "So this is where Grunt lives."

Using a black grease pencil, Dan marked an 'x' on an acetate envelope enclosing a topographic map.

"We'll settle up with you, my friend."

Dan slowly made his way back through the shadows toward his friends.

CHAPTER 16

A RECKONING

Vo Xu, Tucker, and Grunt slept on the ledge by the low fire linked in a shared dream. Tucker had asked Grunt that they sleep outside this last night in the forest. Tucker feared that it would be a long time before he got back into the woods, and truly feared that he would never see Grunt again.

Tucker's eyelids twitched. Vo Xu's legs moved as if running in her sleep. Grunt lay on his back with the images flashing across his unconscious.

Flames encircled the black SUV resting upside down on the hillside adjacent to the blacktop road. The roof of the SUV was compressed pinning Steven and Ann inside. Unconscious, Tucker lay on his side outside the vehicle. Oil and gas seeped from the car and dripped down the earth damp with dew. Jim, Mike, and Dan stood next to the burning vehicle. Jim counted out bills taken from Steven's wallet. Mike rustled through Ann's purse seeking valuables. Dan paced nervously up and down the slope.

Flickering light from the fire washed over Amanda and John as they slept. Black hands holding knives moved from the darkness into the light. Silver blades reflected the red and yellow flames. Blood poured from slit flesh falling onto the ground. Jim and Dan wiped the blood from their knives on the clothes of their victims. Mike chased through the darkness after Tucker.

Shapes, evidenced only by pairs of red eyes, raced through the forest leaving furrows in their wake. They moved swiftly through the trees and across the meadows of the valley. They stopped in the thick woods just across the stream from the old shack.

The Gunpowder River, fed by its smallest tributaries touched with a thin sheet of ice, made its way from the ancient hills on a meandering path to the Hudson River and the sea.

Tucker wrestled uneasily beneath the blanket tormented again by the visitation of the images of death.

Grunt rolled over on his side.

Tucker rose. Vo Xu thrust her head under his shoulder.

"You sweet, sweet girl," Tucker said crying softly into her coat.

Their eyes met. Tucker thought he could see words in Vo Xu's eyes. It was as if she were trying to speak to him.

Vo Xu spun around, and then quickly went down the ladder and disappeared into the night. Tucker sat by the fire pit and looked down. He thought he could see sets of red dots, eyes he imagined, running along with Vo Xu.

Tucker gazed into the weakening wall of night shifting from black to deep gray. His thoughts descended to the well of pain in his soul.

Vo Xu raced to the edge of the clearing, and then ran back to the ladder. As she ascended the ladder Tucker saw an intensity of color in her red eyes he had not witnessed before. Narrow puffs of her hot breath condensed in the crisp morning air. Vo Xu stopped at the top, only her head visible to Tucker. Vo Xu's vision became Tucker's.

Ugly yellow flames ringed the burning SUV. Rivulets of blood flowed from John's punctured body. Grotesquely twisted legs of Ann were held by the vise of the windshield. The campfire's light shone on knife blades slicing deeply into the flesh of John and Amanda.

Tucker saw the Gunpowder River and a shack on the other side of it. He saw three unshaven men in dirty clothes standing before it.

Vo Xu and Tucker's breath joined in a gray cloud. Tucker shook Grunt to wake him.

"They're here! Vo Xo found them! We've got to go! Now!"

"Hold on, hold on," said Grunt. "What are you?"

Grunt looked at Vo Xu. Grunt suddenly connected with the dream.

"Them? The ones?"

Tucker entered the cave, and returned with a bolt action .308 rifle slung over his shoulder.

"And a child shall lead," Grunt said. "Give me that rifle Tucker. It's heavier than you think. Let's go, girl."

Vo Xu led the way down the ladder and the others followed as the sun rose over the trees. Through the thick stand of trees, Tucker watched the Gunpowder River flash and flail as a great white serpent through the dark woods. Eye piercing sunlight reflected from the back of the thundering river.

Vo Xu went forward down the narrow trail. A shiver went down Tucker's spine as he watched Vo Xu go forward across a grass free patch of earth without leaving tracks.

A light snow fell as Tucker and Grunt followed Vo Xu, deeper into the woods. A faint wind tossed the snowflakes into swirling columns, which appeared to move alongside Tucker and the others.

Tucker watched as Vo Xu paused, looked back over her shoulder, waited for him to acknowledge her glance, and then resumed the hunt. Behind Tucker, Grunt strode with the deliberate gait of a soldier eagerly moving toward the sound of the guns.

Tucker gazed, eyes half out of focus, at the swirling columns within the woods parallel to their path.

It's like the soldiers around the campfires. If I stare at them, it's snow. Just blowing snow. If I half look at them, I see them. Shapes, men, arms, legs, and heads.

Tucker listened to the sound of the rushing Gunpowder River. Vo Xu was out of sight up the trail before them, but Tucker's mind's eye was now moving with her. Tucker saw the snow dusted trail making a serpentine passage through the thick woods. He saw Vo Xu poised within the cover of the brush, looking down, and suddenly, Tucker could see them. Pure hate filled Tucker's heart.

Jim, taller than the others, days of stubble on his face, matted hair. He was filthy. Dan and Mike, stumbled and fell on the snow-touched stones in the dry riverbed. Tucker's heart pounded painfully hard. His breathed deeply causing giddiness. Tucker paused catching his breath.

"You all right?" Grunt asked.

"Yeah, just…"

"I know."

Tucker looked at Grunt.

"Tucker, I'm in this with you. But, you got to think real careful, now."

"I did."

Grunt nodded up the trail.

"Be no turning back once it's done."

Tucker nodded to snow draped shapes crouching on their heels within the woods. Grunt followed Tucker's nod.

"Why do you think they're here?"

"Same as you," Grunt said.

"This isn't getting even," Tucker said.

Blood dripping images of Steve, Ann, John, and Amanda came to Tucker.

"This is getting right."

"You sure?" Grunt asked.

"I'm sure,"

Tucker rose, turned from Grunt, and started up the trail.

Grunt reached out, grasped Tucker by the shoulder, and turned him around in mid-stride. Bending down low Grunt looked into Tucker's eyes.

"This is killing," Grunt said.

"Yes, but not murder. Vo Xu is taking us to them."

Tucker looked up the trail again. A strange wind had cleared the snow from the trail, pushed it to the sides, and created pale gray walls on both sides of the trail allowing Tucker a narrow, clear view ahead.

"Let's go."

Swiftly, they closed the distance, the sounds of their approach covered by the noise of the wind and the river.

Tucker watched concealed in the woods as Dan, Jim, and Mike swore at the stones as they slipped and fell making their way across the riverbed to ancient Indian gravesites.

"Look, find my damn wallet, and let's get out of here. We don't want nothing tying us to this place," Jim said.

He and the others leaned their AK47's against rocks.

"Keep it down," Dan said. "I tracked the kid to Grunt's place. He's only a click from here over that ridge."

"If you hadn't dropped the damn thing, we wouldn't be here. Cold as hell."

Mike looked around the narrow gorge.

"Never liked being in this damn place. Something ain't right here."

"Shut up, and find the damn wallet," Jim said," and then we'll settle up with Grunt and the kid."

The three men, bent over, scampered across the stones like so many large rats scurrying from human sight; the stones clattering beneath them.

Tucker and Vo Xu paused out of sight at the edge of the forest overlooking the escarpment as Grunt came up on line. Tucker was the closest to the edge. Tucker looked down upon the three men. Tucker imagined chambering a round and firing the first bullet into the forehead of the tallest killer. Then, turning, he would fire into the hearts of the other two.

After that, thought Tucker, with no heed to the day after, it will be over.

Tucker reached back for the rifle. Grunt took the sling off his shoulder and handed the rifle to Tucker.

Vo Xu slipped into the shadows, ran down the steep slope of the canyon, and paused at the edge. Brush on both sides of her shook though the wind had fallen. Tucker and Grunt moved swiftly down behind her, clinging precariously to tree trunks and limbs to keep from falling.

In front of him, Tucker saw Jim, Dan, and Mike suddenly look up from the ground to see Vo Xu at the edge of the woods. He slipped his arm through the rifle sling and slowly began to raise the barrel.

Vo Xu rose, standing between Tucker and the killers. Slowly, she turned her body, pushing the rifle barrel away. Without a sound, Vo Xu stepped from the darkness of the woods into the light of the canyon. Behind her, first Tucker, and then Grunt stepped into the light.

"What the hell?" Jim shouted.

"The kid," Mike said stepping slowly closer to his rifle on the ground.

The brilliant red of Vo Xu's eyes cast colored tinges on her jowls and her teeth, causing them to glow red. Companion shapes to Vo Xu appeared on both sides of her. The three creatures stepped toward Jim and the others.

Jim was the first to dive to the dry river bed to retrieve a rifle. In an instant, Vo Xu and the others, fangs bared, spine-chilling howls bursting from their lungs, bounded across the rocks.

Jim, Mike, and Dan fired bursts into the air. Vo Xu and the others passed untouched through the hail of fire. Casting down their rifles, Jim ran to the cover of the woods on the opposite bank of the dry riverbed. Mike and Dan followed. Eyes wide and limbs flailing away, the three men clawed their way through the woods and ran down the trail.

Swiftly, Tucker and Grunt ran, reached the woods, and set off after Jim, Dan, and Mike. Vo Xu disappeared into the woods howling.

Ahead, the howling was louder, closer now. Sweat soaked, the cool morning air chilling him, Tucker stood by the bank of the Gunpowder River with Grunt at his side.

Before him, Jim, Dan, and Mike were trapped with their backs against the icy river. In front of them, the woods shook now, with the sound of dozens of creatures of Vo Xu's kind howling. Bared fangs and eyes red with anger appeared.

Jim looked behind him. He saw pieces of windowpane thin ice floating down the swiftly moving river, shattering against rocks. The woods reached the very edge of the river on both sides. Dan and Mike huddled by Jim, shivering.

"Sonofabitch. You!" Jim said to Tucker and Grunt.

"The kid!" shouted Dan. "From that night."

"Shut up, you idiot!" Jim said.

"It don't matter, now," Mike said.

Vo Xu stepped forward raising her head to the sky and slowly opened her mouth. Her long, mournful howl came from deep within her ascending above her and through the treetops. The other creatures joined in; the wail causing the trees and earth to tremble. The three men dropped their rifles.

Tucker was soaked in sweat, his hair matted to his forehead, his buckskins cold and clammy against his flesh. The heavy rifle wavered in his grip as he looked at the three. With all of his strength, Tucker raised the rifle to his shoulder, his shoulder flinching slightly in anticipation of the sharp jerk of the butt into his flesh.

Jim looked desperately to Grunt whose taciturn face provided no hope of clemency. Tucker pointed the rifle at Jim's forehead. Tucker's sweat coated finger pressed lightly against the trigger taking up the slack.

Tucker was truly alone. There was no sound. He owned this moment. Later, Tucker would not be able to say how much time had passed in that moment. As if from a great distance, Tucker heard Jim's words. Tucker saw the SUV carrying himself, Steven, and Ann rolling down the hill and crashing. Tucker saw Jim and Mike slitting the throats of John and Amanda.

"For the love of god, kid!" Jim pleaded.

Vo Xu stepped between the three killers and Tucker. She looked up at Tucker. Tucker lowered the rifle. Grunt reached over and took the weapon from Tucker.

Vo Xu with others of her kind backed up the three men to the edge of the river. The men's feet slipped against the slick bank sending them down into swift, cold water. Vo Xu stopped at the very edge of the river with sharp fangs bared, howling on the riverbank inches from the terrified faces of the men. Pottery shards fell from the pockets of the grave robbers slapping against the white capped surface, and then sinking rapidly to the current swept riverbed.

Tucker watched the men who had murdered his family bobbing in the freezing water; flailing their arms, cursing, and struggling against the numbness in their legs and the certain onset of death.

Mike was the first, sinking below the surface, briefly resurrecting himself with one final lunge from the dark water toward the sky, and then collapsing into the water. Dan died next, slipping under and disappearing.

Finally, Jim, who had watched the others die, slowly sank. His feet slipped across the sandy bottom dragging his chest and head under the water.

Tucker stood silently on the riverbank. Tears streamed down his cheeks and his body shook. Vo Xu stepped to his side. Together, they watched the bodies bob and dip on their course out of the valley striking against boulders as they were pulled by the current. Slowly, the other creatures retreated back into the forest.

"It's over," Tucker said looking at Grunt.

"Let's go," Grunt said.

Tucker turned away from the riverbank with Vo Xu at his side.

"It's done, son."

Grunt placed his hand on Tucker's shoulder and led away from the river.

Without a word Truth, and Grunt with Vo Xu trailing along, made their way back to the cave to pack.

CHAPTER 17
A NEW BEGINNING

It was late in the afternoon when Tucker and Grunt paused inside the cover of the edge of the woods. A cool breeze stirred within the woods rustling their hair and buckskin shirts.

"You sure about this?"

"I'm sure."

"You ready?"

"I'm ready. But, to tell you the truth, I'm afraid."

"We can do this."

"I know we can."

Tucker and Grunt turned and faced the woods which had been Grunt's sanctuary for all those years. Tucker looked up at Grunt.

Grunt's eyes twitched. The muscles of his face tightened. To Tucker it was as if Grunt's face were a movie screen. All of the years Grunt had spent alone in the woods were passing before his eyes. Grunt seemed embarrassed when he looked down and saw Tucker staring at him.

"Never thought I'd leave here. Least ways not alive." Grunt looked through the woods toward the farm field. "You know I'm not sure."

"You backing out?"

"No, young trooper. We got a pact."

Grunt smiled.

The breeze stopped. A pronounced stillness fell upon them all. Nothing moved. There was not a bird in flight nor ripple on a stream nor creature scurrying on the forest floor. The purity of the stillness was consuming. It was as if Tucker and Grunt had found themselves a step inside the cavernous vault of a massive cathedral and the sheer magnetism of it compelled them to take one more step.

It was then that Tucker saw his mother. Anne was there. Smiling, whole, and well. Tears of joy were in her eyes. Tucker heard her say "I love you." Tucker's heart pounded. He thought of going to her, but something deep inside him, instinct, told him not to move. He savored this moment and feared how short it would last.

Then, Tucker saw Steven. His father placed his arm on Anne's shoulder. They were both well.

Tears ran down Tucker's cheeks. He felt Grunt's hand on his shoulder.

"You see them?" Tucker whispered

"Yeah, son. I surely do."

Now, Grandpa John and Grandma Amanda stood by Steven and Ann.

Tucker fell to his knees sobbing in joy. He bent forward and offered a prayer of gratitude. Then, he rose and stood beside Grunt.

Truth and Vo Xu appeared with the others. Tucker looked at Vo Xu and then up to Grunt. A broad smile spread across his face. Grunt nodded.

Tucker looked into Vo Xu's eyes. She was smiling. Tucker knew at that moment that it was Vo Xu who had started all of this. It hit him like a blast almost knocking him off his feet. Tucker pointed at Vo Xu.

"She is…"

"Yeah, I told you about this valley. Healers."

Tucker and Grunt had one long, silent farewell with those they loved, and then they were gone.

"You ready?"

"I'm ready."

Tucker led the way toward the edge of the woods.

"By the way, Who did you pray to?"

Tucker smiled broadly and then laughed.

"It don't matter."

"No, it don't matter."

Together, Tucker and Grunt stepped from the cool shadows of the woods into the sunlit field.

THE END

www.ingramcontent.com/pod-product-compliance
Lightning Source LLC
Chambersburg PA
CBHW020508030426
42337CB00011B/277